CW00840051

The Role of Discourse Analysis for Translation and in Translator Training

CURRENT ISSUES IN LANGUAGE AND SOCIETY

Analysing Political Speeches
Christina Schäffner (ed.)
Children Talking: The Development of Pragmatic Competence
Linda Thompson (ed.)
Cultural Functions of Translation
Christina Schäffner and Helen Kelly-Holmes (eds)
Discourse and Ideologies
Christina Schäffner and Helen Kelly-Holmes (eds)
Ethnicity in Eastern Europe: Questions of Migration, Language Rights and Education
Sue Wright (ed.)
European Television Discourse in Transition
Helen Kelly-Holmes (ed.)
French – an accommodating language? Le français: langue d'accueil?
Sue Wright (ed.)
Language and the State: Revitalization and Revival in Israel and Eire
Sue Wright (ed.)
Language and Conflict: A Neglected Relationship
Sue Wright (ed.)
Language, Democracy and Devolution in Catalonia
Sue Wright (ed.)
Language Policy and Language Issues in the Successor States of the Former USSR
Sue Wright (ed.)
Languages in Contact and Conflict: Contrasting Experiences in the Netherlands and Belgium
Sue Wright (ed.)
Managing Language Diversity
Sue Wright and Helen Kelly-Holmes (eds)
Managing Multilingualism in a European Nation-State: Challenges for Sweden
Sally Boyd and Leena Huss (eds)
Minority Language Broadcasting: Breton and Irish
Helen Kelly-Holmes (ed.)
Monolingualism and Bilingualism: Lessons from Canada and Spain
Sue Wright (ed.)
One Country, Two Systems, Three Languages: A Survey of Changing Language Use in Hong Kong
Sue Wright and Helen Kelly-Holmes (eds)
Translation and Quality
Christina Schäffner (ed.)
Translation and Norms
Christina Schäffner (ed.)
Translation in the Global Village
Christina Schäffner (ed.)

Other Books of Interest
Contemporary Translation Theories (2nd Edition)
Edwin Gentzler
Literary Translation: A Practical Guide
Clifford E. Landers
Practical Guide for Translators
Geoffrey Samuelsson-Brown

Please contact us for the latest book information:
Multilingual Matters, Frankfurt Lodge, Clevedon Hall,
Victoria Road, Clevedon, BS21 7HH, England
http://www.multilingual-matters.com

The Role of Discourse Analysis for Translation and in Translator Training

Edited by

Christina Schäffner

MULTILINGUAL MATTERS LTD
Clevedon • Buffalo • Toronto • Sydney

Library of Congress Cataloging in Publication Data
A catalog record for this book is available from the Library of Congress.

British Library Cataloguing in Publication Data
A catalogue entry for this book is available from the British Library.

ISBN 1-85359-593-4 (hbk)

Multilingual Matters Ltd
UK: Frankfurt Lodge, Clevedon Hall, Victoria Road, Clevedon BS21 7HH.
USA: UTP, 2250 Military Road, Tonawanda, NY 14150, USA.
Canada: UTP, 5201 Dufferin Street, North York, Ontario M3H 5T8, Canada.
Australia: Footprint Books, PO Box 418, Church Point, NSW 2103, Australia.

This book is also available as Vol. 7, No. 3 of the journal *Current Issues in Language and Society.*

Printed and bound in Great Britain by Short Run Press Ltd.

Contents

Editorial
Discourse Analysis for Translation and Translator Training: Status, Needs, Methods

Christina Schäffner
Institute for the Study of Language and Society, Aston University, Birmingham B4 7ET, UK

Introduction

The discipline of Translation Studies is becoming increasingly recognised as a discipline in its own right, having outgrown such disciplines as (applied) linguistics and/or comparative literature to which it was originally seen to belong. However, the concepts (or terms) we use to speak about translation are concepts that originate from linguistics and its neighbouring disciplines. In the course of time, some of these concepts have been modified (e.g. the notion of the 'unit of translation'), others have been added on (e.g. 'skopos', 'loyalty', 'ethics'), but only rarely have concepts been completely discarded (as reflected in the controversies about the term 'equivalence', for example). Such conceptual developments are evidence of the increasing awareness of the complexity of translation as both a cognitive and a social activity, which cannot be fully explained by reference to concepts derived from (structural) linguistics only. It has also to be acknowledged, however, that over the last 50 years, the very discipline of linguistics has undergone developments too. The main object of research of linguistics is no longer the language system qua system (cf. de Saussure's (1959) *langue*), but also aspects of how language is actually used in various communicative situations, and how contextual, generic, cognitive, sociocultural, historical, ideological, etc. factors influence structures and functions of language in use, and vice versa. In linguistics, these developments are reflected in labels such as textlinguistics, sociolinguistics, psycholinguistics, cognitive linguistics, critical linguistics, etc. which indicate the focus of the new sub-disciplines (although it could be argued whether they indeed constitute sub-disciplines of linguistics or rather disciplines in their own right).

These developments have also had an impact on Translation Studies, with the discipline adopting and, where necessary, modifying concepts and methods from textlinguistics, sociolinguistics, psycholinguistics, etc. (cf. Neubert & Shreve, 1992: 12ff. on various models of translation, also Munday 2001, Stolze 1997). Recently, concepts and analytical methods from other disciplines have also become more prominent in speaking about translation, most notably from Cultural Studies and Anthropology, which again have added to our insights into the phenomenon of translation as an activity and the role translations as products play in and for society. Translation Studies by its very nature can thus be characterised as an interdiscipline (cf. Snell-Hornby *et al.*, 1992).

Speaking about translation with reference to concepts and methods derived from linguistics, text- and sociolinguistics, pragmatics and discourse analysis, however, has a very strong tradition both in the discipline of Translation Studies itself and in translator training. One of the main reasons being that there is general agreement that understanding a text is a prerequisite for translating it, i.e. for producing a target text (TT) on the basis of a source text (ST). Understanding includes reflecting about the linguistic structures which a text displays, realising that the structure chosen by the text producer is (to be) seen as the most appropriate one to fulfil the intended aims and purposes which the author wanted to achieve with the text for specific communicative situations in a specific sociocultural context for specific addressees. A systematic text analysis therefore figures prominently in many textbooks about translation, but the actual methods suggested and the concepts used vary.

A closer look at any one particular model, i.e. its aim, content, application, achievement, would therefore provide useful information and inspiration for everybody involved in translator training. This was the purpose of a seminar held at Aston University in November 2000 which was devoted to discussing the role of Discourse Analysis for translation and translator training. The main contributor to the seminar, and subsequently to this issue, is Anna Trosborg from the Aarhus School of Business (Denmark), who has published widely in the fields of discourse and genre analysis, text typology and translation (cf. for example, Trosborg, 1997, 1997b, 2000). In her position paper, she presents a model of discourse analysis which includes elements which have been derived from a number of linguistic (sub-)disciplines. Trosborg explains the elements of her model in detail, and illustrates its application with reference to one particular sample text. Students' translations, preceded by comments on how they applied the model to the ST and followed by comments on their translations were presented at the seminar, and summarised in the position paper. In the subsequent debate, and also in the response papers, the content of Trosborg's model and aspects of its application are discussed, often in a critical way. Major issues concern terminological choices, the elements of the model, and the required depth of analysis in the specific context of translator training.

Terminology

This volume reflects a general agreement that some kind of analysis of the ST is an indispensable phase in the translation process. Equally there is agreement that text analysis should be taught and practised in translator training courses. However, there is less agreement as to the depth of analysis and, in relation to this, to the actual elements of a model of analysis. In her position paper, Anna Trosborg describes in detail a model she has been using in her own classes for a number of years. In the first part of her paper, she presents and defines the elements of the model. As she explains, her approach is largely based on Halliday's register analysis (e.g. Halliday, 1978) and also on genre analysis (e.g. Bhatia, 1993; Martin, 1984; Swales, 1990), but her model is essentially an eclectic one. As Trosborg argues, using theoretical concepts from various linguistic (sub-)disciplines, instead of adhering strictly to one particular theory, allows for a deeper understanding of the text. One consequence of borrowing concepts (or terms) from different disciplines or from different scholars may be terminological confusion. As is very often the case in linguistics, but also in other disciplines, there is no general agreement about specific terms, and this became obvious at the Aston seminar as well. Trosborg uses discourse analysis and text analysis, she speaks of discourse, text, text type, genre, register – terms that come with their own history – and both the debate and the response papers seem to reflect different understandings of these terms. I will only illustrate such terminological differences with respect to the pairs 'discourse' and 'text', and 'text type' and 'genre'.

Focusing on language in use became more prominent in the late 1960s/early 1970s, when scholars from various countries and from different disciplinary backgrounds began to study regularities in structures beyond the sentence level, also studying written and spoken forms of language in use. 'Text' and 'discourse' were often used as synonyms, but some scholars preferred to speak of 'text' for the written mode and of 'discourse' for the oral mode (e.g. the term 'discourse analysis' is often used for analysing spoken interaction and turn-taking mechanisms, with this analytical method also referred to as 'conversation analysis', 'ethnomethodology' (for a summary see Bublitz, 1991; Georgakopoulou & Goutsos, 1997; van Dijk, 1997). In other cases, 'text' is used for an individual piece of (written or oral) communication, and 'discourse' then denotes a sequence of texts which belong together due to a common subject domain (e.g. the discourse on right-wing extremism), or due to a single author (e.g. the discourse of Margaret Thatcher). Notions such as 'intertextuality' and 'interdiscursivity' have their origin in such aspects (Fairclough, 1995).

Although Trosborg does not provide an explicit definition, neither of the term 'discourse' nor that of 'text', it becomes clear from her presentation that she sees text as the unit for discourse analysis, which is in line with the Hallidayan tradition. She speaks of 'text' with reference to an individual, concrete occurrence, whereas 'discourse' applies to a higher level and involves regular patterns in the use of language by social groups in areas of sociocultural activity. This is reflected in the notions of field, tenor, and mode of discourse. Identifying personal pronouns in a text, for example, would be part of reflecting on the tenor of discourse, based on Halliday and applied by Trosborg. In a communicatively and functionally oriented textlinguistic approach, as outlined in de Beaugrande and Dressler (1981), personal pronouns could be studied with reference to their seven standards of textuality, here specifically intentionality and/or cohesion. Or, Halliday and Hasan's (1990) field of discourse refers to the total event in which the text is functioning, which would come under the standard of situationality in de Beaugrande and Dressler's framework. Adding these standards of textuality to Trosborg's model (see Adab's response paper) would therefore not add anything substantially new, but only change the perspective.

'Text type' and 'genre', too, are sometimes used as synonyms, but they are more often treated as separate entities. The terminological confusion here is related to attempts to classify texts. Various criteria, both text-external and text-internal, have been used to arrive at a typology of texts. Some typologies are based on a dominant communicative function, or the communicative purpose, of the text (e.g. Isenberg, 1984; Werlich, 1975). In such a perspective, scholars have usually set up a limited number of categories. For example, Werlich's typology has five idealised text types (description, narration, exposition, argumentation, instruction) or, with specific relevance to Translation Studies, the three types of Katharina Reiss (1971, 1976) – informative, expressive, operative.

These basic text types are then linked to specific genres or text varieties (Reiss, 1971). In German textlinguistic literature, 'Texttyp' (text type) is understood as a category for a more abstract, theoretical classification of texts, and 'Textsorte' (or 'Textklasse', i.e. genre, text class, text variety) is a label used for an empirical classification of texts as they exist in a human society (cf. Heinemann & Viehweger, 1991: 144). 'Textsorte' corresponds to what is typically called 'genre' in Anglo-Saxon studies on genre analysis. Genres ('Textsorten') are defined as global linguistic patterns which have historically developed in a linguistic community for fulfilling specific communicative tasks in specific situations. Genres reflect the effective, conscious and situationally appropriate choice of linguistic means. Members of a linguistic community therefore have specific genre knowledge, rather than text-type knowledge (cf. Heinemann & Viehweger, 1991: 144; see also Trosborg, 1997a; Schäffner, 2000a).

Genres are embedded in sociologically determined communicative activities. They can be described as conventional, typical combinations of contextual (situational) or communicative–functional, and structural (grammatical and thematic) features. It is in this respect that genres, rather than text types, have become relevant for Translation Studies. Due to their (more or less) conventional structures, genres can provide some orientation for the production of texts, including translation as text production.

In her model, Trosborg does not use 'genre' in this sense as is widely accepted in the discipline of Translation Studies. However, she sees genre as the overall purpose of an interaction and as superordinate to register features. The term 'register', then, is used to describe the immediate situational context in which a text is produced, referring to field, tenor and mode as the three areas of text realisation. Most of the participants at the Aston seminar had problems following Trosborg in her use of the terms, and Dimitriu and Zlateva take up this issue again in their response papers. Trosborg's use of the terms reflects her own disciplinary background: a genre and register analyst in the tradition of Halliday's and Swales' approach to translation; in contrast to a translation scholar who is looking to linguistics, genre analysis, etc. in order to find concepts and methods of analysis which could prove useful to speak about translation.

As stated earlier, terminological differences are quite common in our discipline and once the terms have been clearly defined, it is possible to discuss their value for application. With respect to the components of the model presented by Trosborg, i.e. the actual content of the model irrespective of controversial definitions of individual terms, the question is: which concepts and analytical methods are useful for the process of translation and for translator training? Trosborg's model is very extensive, it contains a number of elements which have been adopted from, among others, (lexical) semantics (e.g. notions such as meaning, taxonomy, frame), pragmatics (e.g. speech acts, presupposition) and stylistics. We can obviously discuss whether there is too much in the proposed model or whether some elements are missing (see the Debate which follows Trosborg's paper), but the contents of a model would need to be chosen in view of its purpose. In other words, what is to be achieved by a model of discourse analysis, and specifically in the context of translator training?

Why and How to Do Discourse Analysis for Translation?

Whether we call it discourse analysis for translation, as Trosborg does, translation-oriented ST analysis (e.g. Nord, 1991) or pre-translational text analysis (e.g. Erdmann *et al.*, 1994), the aim is, in general, identical: to identify specific textual features which are relevant for the process of translation. The problem, however, is that such an analysis needs to be fully understood as a translation-oriented analysis, and not as a text analysis in its own right; that is, text and/or discourse analysis can be done for various purposes, e.g. as part of a seminar on textlinguistics, where the aim of the analysis could be to identify theme/rheme progression in a text, or to see how the logical flow of some topic or argument (coherence) is reflected in the textual surface structure (cohesion). A text can also be analysed from a comparative perspective, for example in order to find what the conventions are of a particular genre (such as instruction manuals, annual business reports, editorials in a newspaper) in a specific culture and how these compare to the genre conventions in another culture. Depending on the purpose of such an analysis, the focus will differ, as will the required depth of analysis.

ST analysis as a phase in the translation process has its own specific purpose: to identify and highlight 'specific textual features which might be expected to present translation problems in order to steer translation decisions' (Erdmann *et al.*, 1994: 4). The partly controversial debate at the Aston seminar was due to a widespread impression that the model presented by Trosborg was aimed at a detailed linguistic analysis of the text as such, but that it did not sufficiently account for the fact that it is an analysis for translation (this issue has been taken up again in almost all of the response papers). What I would like to add is that there is obviously a danger in presenting a model by listing all its elements in a kind of list (see the Appendix to Trosborg's paper) which the students are encouraged to follow and to write answers to each of the items mentioned. The danger I see is that students become too occupied with 'working through' the list, looking too closely at the ST in order to find examples for each element on the list, and forgetting that they are doing this with a view to translating the text, and not just analysing for the sake of analysis (and we have to remind ourselves that the model is intended for use in the classroom, with students of translation, who are at the stage of advanced beginners in their developmental process (cf. Chesterman, 1997, 2000, following Dreyfus & Dreyfus, 1986). In other words, the model seems to suggest a text analysis in its own right and, moreover, it seems to encourage a bottom-up approach, rather than a top-down approach. It needs to be acknowledged that Trosborg's model (see the Appendix) starts with the extratextual features, but the by far more extensive part requests detailed information about the intratextual features.

Another reason why it was generally felt that the model does not sufficiently allow for a translation-oriented text analysis is the fact that comments about the skopos are requested only following the ST analysis (as part B of the model, see the Appendix). Although Trosborg has explicitly stated in her position paper that her approach to translation is built on skopos theory (Reiss & Vermeer, 1991), and specifically on Nord's interpretation and development of skopos theory (e.g. Nord, 1991, 1997), the actual sequence of the various steps in the model remained unclear (but see Trosborg's comments in her reply to the responses where she elaborates on this point). Moreover, the papers by the students, which were used for illustration at the Aston seminar, actually seemed to confirm the impression that the text analysis was done with insufficient attention to translation. In these papers, for example, comments about skopos, the purpose of the TT and about translation decisions were made primarily with reference to the ST. Actually asking for a detailed analysis of the translation brief and the TT skopos as a first item in the students' papers might help to focus their analysis (cf. Holz-Mänttäri's initial steps of 'Bedarfserfassung' [need specification] and 'Produktspezifikation' [product specification] [Holz-Mänttäri, 1984]; see also Vienne [2000] and the response papers by Adab and Millán-Varela in this volume). The most important point is that students, as trainee translators, become sensitised to recognise linguistic structures in texts, that they learn to reflect on the specific function of textual structures for the overall purpose of the text in a communicative context, and that, based on such reflections, they will be able to make informed decisions as to the linguistic structures required for the TT in the new context and culture for new addressees.

In the context of university training, it may be pedagogically useful to focus initially more on the text analysis and bring in the translation focus in a second step. Students often (want to) start translating immediately, without a more conscious reflection about the text and their task. Whether such an initial 'backstepping' from the translation focus is advisable or not depends, to a large extent, on the overall syllabus of the translation training programme. As Trosborg illustrates, her module is one which combines text and discourse analysis and translation, that is, students are made familiar with linguistic concepts and methods of analysis. In such a context, her approach is certainly useful (and her results over the years seem to confirm this). In university programmes, where modules on linguistics, text and discourse analysis are elementary parts of the curriculum, the translation modules can build on knowledge and thus focus fully on a translation-oriented analysis. There was general agreement at the Aston seminar that knowledge of linguistic concepts and methods is highly relevant for translation practice. In fact, linguistic competence is an essential element of translation competence (which is a complex notion and includes additional sub-competences, for example, cultural competence, textual competence, domain/subject specific competence, (re)search competence, transfer competence, see Schäffner, 2000b; Neubert, 2000 and the contributions in Schäffner & Adab, 2000).

Do we Need Models?

Despite the general agreement that methods of discourse analysis should be included in translator training programmes, the questions of how exactly this should be done and to what extent it should be practised remain. Several colleagues objected in this respect to the use of the label 'model' and suggested 'approach' instead (see the Debate, and also the response papers by Adab and Zlateva). There are a few points I wish to make: first, if we say that a 'model' actually represents what happens in reality, then Trosborg's model is not a model. It does not represent the actual nature and sequence of a process of text analysis –

but neither is it presented or intended as such by Trosborg. Second, if we require that the term 'model' is only used if we are operating strictly within one particular theory, then again, Trosborg's model is not a model since it is eclectic, drawing from various theories. Third, we need to remind ourselves that Trosborg speaks of a model of textual analysis, and not of a model of translation (i.e. she does not relate her arguments to models of translation as discussed, for example, by Neubert & Shreve, 1992). Some of the comments during the debate regarding missing elements in the model seem to have been made with a view to a model for approaching a translation task, where discourse analysis would be one element. In her concluding comments, Trosborg argues that translation theories should formulate a set of strategies for approaching problems and for coordinating the different aspects entailed. Her own model can be seen as a step towards formulating strategies, its focus is on the identification of textual features as a precondition of approaching translation problems (as stated earlier, this aim of the model will probably require a re-balancing of its elements). And finally, if we define 'model' in the sense of a tool (which, I think, is the sense Trosborg intended), then we can focus on its practical use (and we may as well stick to the label 'model' – a label which has also been used by Nord, 1988 and Hönig, 1986, who both speak of a 'model of translation relevant text analysis'). Seen as a tool, we have an orientational framework which can be used independently of the specific language pair, the text type and/or genre, and the translation direction.

A translation-oriented ST analysis, whether on the basis of the model suggested by Trosborg, or on the basis of a (more or less) different 'model', or 'approach', is intended to heighten students' awareness of the processes involved in translating and in the production of translations. It will help them to reflect on what they are doing, and it will also provide them with arguments and terms to use when commenting on their translation decisions. It is a tool for developing translation competence.

References

Bhatia, V.K. (1993) Analysing genre. *Language Use in Professional Settings.* London/New York: Longman.

Bublitz, W. (1991) Discourse analysis: The state of the art. In C. Uhlig and R. Zimmermann (eds) *Anglistentag 1990 Marburg Proceedings* (pp. 259–84). Tübingen: Niemeyer.

Chesterman, A. (1997) *Memes of Translation.* Amsterdam and Philadelphia: Benjamins.

Chesterman, A. (2000) Teaching strategies for emancipatory translation. In C. Schäffner and B. Adab (eds) *Developing Translation Competence* (pp. 77–90). Amsterdam and Philadelphia: Benjamins.

de Beaugrande, R.A. and Dressler, U.D. (1981) *Introduction to Text Linguistics.* London: Longman.

Dreyfus, H.L. and Dreyfus, S.E. (1986) *Mind over Machine.* Oxford: Blackwell.

Erdmann, R., Horton, D., Lauer, A. and Steiner, E. (1994) *Perspectives on Pre-translational Text Analysis.* (L.A.U.D. series, Paper no. 343). Duisburg: Linguistic Agency University of Duisburg.

Fairclough, N. (1995) *Critical Discourse Analysis.* London: Longman.

Georgakopoulou, A. and Goutsos, D. (1997) *Discourse Analysis. An Introduction.* Edinburgh: Edinburgh University Press.

Halliday, M.A.K. (1978) *Language as Social Semiotic: The Social Interpretation of Language and Meaning.* London: Edward Arnold.

Halliday, M.A.K. and Hasan, R. (1990) *Cohesion in English* (10th edn). London: Longman.

Heinemann, W. and Viehweger, D. (1991) *Textlinguistik. Eine Einführung* (Germanistische Linguistik 115). Tübingen: Niemeyer.

Holz-Mänttäri, J. (1984) *Translatorisches Handeln. Theorie und Methode.* Helsinki: Suomalainen Tiedeakatemia.

Hönig, H. (1986) Übersetzen zwischen Reflex und Reflexion – ein Modell der übersetzungsrelevanten Textanalyse. In M. Snell-Hornby (ed.) *Übersetzungswissenschaft. Eine Neuorientierung* (pp. 230–51). Tübingen: Franke.

Isenberg, H. (1984) Texttypen als Interaktionstypen. *Zeitschrift für Germanistik* 5 (2), 261–70.

Martin, J.R. (1984) Language, register and genre. In F. Christie (ed.) *Children Writing: Reader* (pp. 21–29). Geelong, Vic: Deakin University Press.

Munday, J. (2001) *Introducing Translation Studies. Theories and Applications.* London and New York: Routledge.

Neubert, A. (2000) Competence in language, in languages, and in translation. In C. Schäffner and B. Adab (eds) *Developing Translation Competence* (pp. 3–18). Amsterdam and Philadelphia: Benjamins.

Neubert, A. and Shreve, G.M. (1992) *Translation as Text.* Kent and London: Kent State University Press.

Nord, C. (1988) *Textanalyse und Übersetzen.* Heidelberg: Groos.

Nord, C. (1991) *Text Analysis in Translation.* Amsterdam: Rodopi.

Nord, C. (1997) *Translating as a Purposeful Activity. Functionalist Approaches Explained.* Manchester: St. Jerome.

Reiss, K. (1971) *Möglichkeiten und Grenzen der Übersetzungskritik.* München: Hueber.

Reiss, K. (1976) *Texttyp und Übersetzungsmethode. Der operative Text.* Kronberg: Scriptor.

Reiss, K. and Vermeer, H.J. (1991) *Grundlegung einer allgemeinen Translationstheorie* (= Linguistische Arbeiten 147) (2nd edn). Tübingen: Niemeyer.

de Saussure, F. (1959) *Course in General Linguistics* (C. Bally and A. Sechehaye, eds). New York: The Philosophical Library.

Schäffner, C. (2000a) The role of genre for translation. In A. Trosborg (ed.) *Analysing Professional Genres* (pp. 209–24). Amsterdam and Philadelphia: Benjamins.

Schäffner, C. (2000b) Running before walking? Designing a translation programme at undergraduate level. In C. Schäffner and B. Adab (eds) *Developing Translation Competence* (pp. 143–56). Amsterdam and Philadelphia: Benjamins.

Schäffner, C. and Adab, B. (eds) (2000) *Developing Translation Competence.* Amsterdam and Philadelphia: Benjamins.

Snell-Hornby, M., Pöchhacker, F. and Kaindl, K. (eds) (1992) *Translation Studies. An Interdiscipline.* Amsterdam and Philadelphia: Benjamins.

Stolze, R. (1997) *Übersetzungstheorien. Eine Einführung* (2nd edn). Tübingen: Narr.

Swales, J.M. (1990) *Genre Analysis. English in Academic and Research Settings.* Cambridge: Cambridge University Press.

Trosborg, A. (1997a) Text typology: Register, genre and text type. In A. Trosborg (ed.) *Text Typology and Translation* (pp. 3–23). Amsterdam and Philadelphia: Benjamins.

Trosborg, A. (ed.) (1997b) *Text Typology and Translation.* Amsterdam and Philadelphia: Benjamins.

Trosborg, A. (ed.) (2000) *Analysing Professional Genres.* Amsterdam and Philadelphia: Benjamins.

van Dijk, T.A. (1997) The study of discourse. In T.A. van Dijk (ed.) *Discourse Studies. A Multidisciplinary Introduction. Vol. 1: Discourse as Structure and Process* (pp. 1–34). London: Sage.

Vienne, J. (2000) Which competences should we teach to future translators, and how? In C. Schäffner and B. Adab (eds) *Developing Translation Competence* (pp. 91–100). Amsterdam and Philadelphia: Benjamins.

Werlich, E. (1975) *Typologie der Texte.* Heidelberg: Quelle & Meyer.

Discourse Analysis as Part of Translator Training

Anna Trosborg
The Aarhus School of Business, Department of English, Fuglesangsallé 4, DK-8210 Aarhus V, Denmark

This paper presents an approach to textual analysis and its application in translator training for university students at advanced level at the Aarhus School of Business. The course is voluntary and is aimed at students who are interested in in-depth textual analysis that is translation oriented. Its approach is to create a deep understanding of the source text (ST) by means of a detailed analysis of it. Understanding the text in full gives the translator a thorough overview and the possibility of maintaining or adapting the ST in a conscious way to meet the demands of the target text (TT) skopos when producing the TT. The approach emphasises not only the quality of the product (the translation) but also how the process is administered. Thus, we are dealing with a process-oriented approach to translation. It draws on the ideas and work of a number of theorists. The main source is Halliday's register analysis, as administered by a number of scholars (e.g. Hatim & Mason, Baker, Eggins, Butt *et al.*), but the work of researchers in speech act theory, genre analysis and semantic theory also play a part. An eclectic approach has been chosen as the aim has been to bring in theoretical aspects that contribute to a deeper understanding of the text regardless of a strict adherence to one particular theory. This approach to translation is built on skopos theory relying on Nord's interpretation of Reiss and Vermeer's ideas about skopos. Part I of this paper outlines the approach to textual analysis. Part 2 applies the approach to one particular text. Part 3 is concerned with translation strategies in general and in relation to the particular text chosen.

Introduction

This paper presents an approach to textual analysis used as part of translator training for the teaching of university students at advanced level at the Aarhus School of Business. The course is voluntary and is aimed at students who are interested in in-depth textual analysis that is translation-oriented. The course is taught over two semesters followed by a one-week written assignment: 12–15 pages of textual analysis and translation of a given text. Textual analysis and translation have equal weight in the grading of a student's work and is given an equal amount of attention during the course. As such, the course offers special opportunities for making detailed analyses of texts before translating, which is a luxury rarely possible in ordinary translation classes because it is too time-consuming.

The aim of the approach is to achieve an in-depth understanding of the source text (ST) through a detailed analysis. Understanding the text in full gives the translator a thorough overview and the possibility of maintaining or adapting the ST in a conscious way to meet the demands of the target text (TT) skopos. It must also be noted that the approach emphasises not only the quality of the product (the translation) but also how the process is administered. Thus we are dealing with a process-oriented approach to translation.

The approach to be presented here draws on the ideas and work of a number of theorists. The main source is M.A.K. Halliday's register analysis, as implemented by a number of scholars (e.g. Baker, 1992; Butt *et al.*, 1995; Eggins, 1994; Hatim & Mason, 1990); but the work of researchers in speech act theory, genre analysis and semantic theory also plays a part. An eclectic approach has been chosen, as the aim has been to bring in theoretical aspects that contribute to a deeper understanding of the text regardless of a strict adherence to one particular theory. This approach to translation is built on the skopos theory relying on Christiane Nord's (see, e.g. Nord, 1991, 1997) interpretation of Reiss and Vermeer's (1984) ideas about skopos.

The aim of this paper is:

- to present and discuss the model
- to evaluate student papers utilising the model
- to assess the validity of the model with a view to its improvement and hence to improving the quality of student education.

A short outline of the approach is enclosed as the Appendix.

Part 1 outlines the approach to textual analysis. Part 2 applies the approach to one particular text: 'Not Quite Across the Rubicon' (in *The Economist*, 27 February 1999, *Bagehot* section). This text can be downloaded from the web (www.economist.com). Part 3 is concerned with translation strategies (1) in general, and (2) in relation to this particular text.

Part I: Approach to Textual Analysis

In this part, I will introduce and explain the theoretical concepts used in the textual analysis, thereby relating them to relevant literature where these concepts are used in similar or different ways.

1.1 Extra-textual features

1.1.1 Situational aspects

(a) *Place of communication:* The parameter of place may be of significance for the understanding of a text. Where in the English-speaking world was it produced and published? A clarification of that may lead to a general awareness of the meaning of certain words and structures, cultural aspects, etc.

(b) *Time of communication:* The parameter of time may also lead to a better understanding of a text. If, for example, a non-contemporary text is to be translated, it may be of importance to be able to identify expressions and slang from a certain era, partly to be able to understand the text, partly to be able to translate it for a new recipient group.

(c) *Context of situation:* This concept was formulated 1923 by Malinowski in his supplement to Ogden and Richards' *The Meaning of Meaning*. It was subsequently elaborated by Firth (1951) and extended in a number of studies, the best-known treatment perhaps being Hymes' (1971) discussion of models of the interaction between language and social setting. Hymes categorises the speech situation in terms of eight components which Halliday and Hasan summarise as: form and content of text, setting, participants, ends (intent and effect), key, medium, genre and interactional norms (Halliday & Hasan, 1990: 22).

A more abstract interpretation has been offered in *The Linguistic Sciences and Language Teaching* by Halliday *et al.* (1964), who proposed the three headings of *field, tenor* and *mode* as a basis for deriving the features of the text from the features of the situation (Halliday & Hasan, 1990: 22). It must be noted that Halliday and Hasan emphasise that these components are highly general concepts for describing how the context of situation determines the kinds of meaning that are expressed, whereas in Hymes' view, the text itself forms part of the speech situation.

According to Halliday and Hasan, the context of situation, which refers to what is going on in the specific situation in which the text occurs, is given substance in the words and grammatical patterns of the text. The situational differences between texts may be accounted for by the three aspects of context, i.e. field, tenor and mode. For Halliday and Hasan (1990: 22), these aspects collectively define the context of situation of a text. *Field* refers to the total event in which the text is functioning, together with the purposive activity of the speaker or writer, thus including the subject matter as one element in it. *Tenor* refers to the type of role interactions, the set of relevant social relations, permanent and temporary, among the participants involved. *Mode* refers to the function of the text in the event and includes the channel taken by the language (spoken or written, extempore or prepared).

In a number of studies, the framework introduced by Halliday, McIntosh and Strevens has formed a theoretical basis for specifying the components of a speech situation. The notion of field has given rise to some discussion. According to Baker (1992: 16), *field of discourse* is an abstract term for 'what is going on' that is relevant to the speaker's choice of linguistic items. The immediate action of speaking in which speakers see themselves as participating will determine linguistic choices. Consequently, linguistic choices will vary according to activity: for example, it will make a difference whether the speaker is taking part in a football match or discussing football; making love or discussing love; making a political speech or discussing politics; performing an operation or discussing medicine (Baker, 1992: 16).

Hatim and Mason (1990), who also distinguish field, tenor, and mode as the three basic aspects of register, endeavour to point out that field and subject matter are not identical. We are likely to encounter fields that are characterised by a variety of subject matters; for example, political discourse as a field may be about law and order, taxation or foreign policy. Only when the subject matter is highly predictable in a given situation (e.g. a physics lecture) or when it is constitutive of a given social activity (e.g. a courtroom interaction) can we legitimately recognise a close link between field and subject matter (Hatim & Mason, 1990: 48).

Tenor of discourse is an abstract term for the relationship between people taking part in the discourse. The language that people use varies depending on interpersonal role relationships, whether they are symmetrical, i.e. the two parties are equals, or asymmetrical, i.e. one party has a superior or inferior status in relation to the other party. Status, age and knowledge are crucial factors. An asymmetrical relationship is said to hold between specialist and layman, as, for example, between doctor and patient, parent and child, teacher and pupil, employer and employee, etc. As such, *tenor* refers to the role relationship between the addresser and the addressee and may be termed 'interpersonal tenor'.

Mode of discourse is an abstract term for the role that language plays, especially as a consequence of its mode (or medium) of transmission (spoken or written). The medium is characterised as simple if language stays within one mode, for example 'written to be read'; or it is characterised as complex if the there is a change of mode, for example 'written to be read as if spoken'. The complex medium is used as a means to an end rather than as an end in itself; the category is conceived as a temporary device meant to facilitate a later switch to the alternative category (see House, 1981: 40).

Furthermore, Martin (1984) has suggested that the role of mode can be seen as involving two simultaneous continua which describe two different types of distance in the relation between language and situation: *spatial/interpersonal distance* and *experiential distance*. The first continuum of spatial/interpersonal distance ranges situations according to the possibilities of immediate feedback between the actors. At one pole of the continuum is the situation of sitting down to a casual chat with friends, where there is both visual and aural contact, and feedback is immediate. At the other end of the continuum would be the situation of writing a book, where there is no visual or aural contact between writer and reader(s), and thus no possibility of immediate feedback. In between these two poles we can situate other types of situation such as telephone calls, radio broadcasts as well as modern communication modes (faxes, telexes, electronic mail, etc.).

The second continuum of experiential distance ranges situations according to the distance between language and the social process occurring. At one pole of this continuum, we have situations such as playing a game (cards, monopoly, etc.) where language is being used to accompany the activity in which interactants are involved. The other polar extreme could be the writing of a piece of fiction or the drafting of a legal document. There is no social process going on, as language is, in fact creating, and therefore constituting, the social process. The language accompanying the process is seen as language as action, while language as constituting the social process is seen as language as reflection. For further development on this point, see Martin (1984, 1985) and Eggins (1994).

If we combine these two dimensions of mode – spatial/interpersonal distance and experiential distance (by taking the end points of each continuum) – we can characterise the basic contrast between spoken and written situations of language use, which result in the well-known differences between written and spoken language.

Hatim and Mason (1990: 49) include genre (letter, essay, poem, advertisement, etc.) as part of the mode. Note that in my approach, genre is not treated as part of the mode, neither is it part of the field. Instead genre is seen as the overall purpose of the interaction and thus super-ordinate to register features. A genre is representative of a text as a whole and an advertisement, for example, refers to the whole text, not to a component of the text, be it field or mode.

Social context refers to the many domains about which discourse analysis can provide relevant insights: racist reporting in the news media, the enactment of power in and by the discourses of authorities, the inequities arising from the prevalence of white middle-class discourse styles in multi-ethnic schools, the use of sexist discourse, etc.

The constraints of the various features of the social context, such as gender, status, power, ethnicity roles or institutional settings, on the interpretation of a text, its thematic structure, its choices with regard to lexis, etc. are also important.

However, many of the observations we make in the area of social context are limited by the fact that we simply do not yet know enough about the importance of many linguistic features in, for instance, a job interview, a court trial, a TV programme, etc. However, we know quite a lot about contextual constraints such as dominance, the power, the status or the ethnocentrism of participants in a communicative event, at least in our mother tongue. The interesting point then is to identify such elements in an English text, and to be able to 'copy' them in a relevant way in a translation.

The ideas presented here may be illustrated as in Figure 1. Note that the figure also includes the notion of genre to be further explained in the next section.

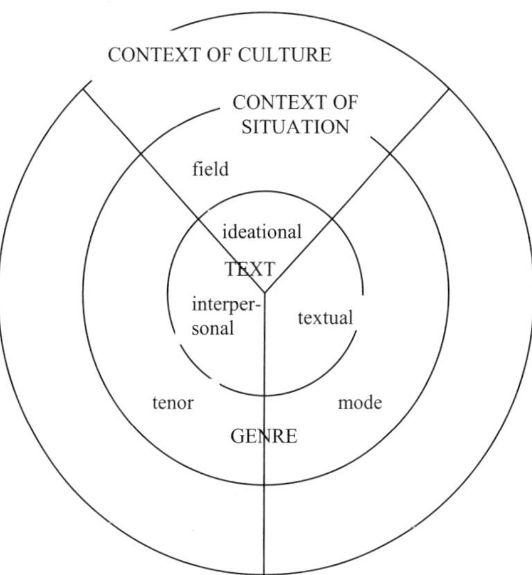

Figure 1 Contextual variables

1.1.2 Genre

Genre analysis has been concerned with establishing the characteristics of particular types of texts. Discourse plays a crucial role in ideological formulation in laws, meetings, media coverage, informal daily talk, the formulation of documents, etc., but whereas the concept of genre has a long tradition in literary studies, interest in the analysis of non-literary texts is of more recent date. It is only throughout the last decade or so that genre analysis has become popular in non-fictional texts.

With the work of Swales (1990) and Bhatia (1993), a framework was established which should prove useful for research in Language for Specific Purposes and business communication. Swales found that sets of texts recognised by the community as members of the same genre showed certain predictable regularities, and his analysis of the research article has become a stepping-stone for further research. Genres are defined through their communicative purposes and obligatory moves, which capture the structure, can be identified. These moves depend on rhetorical strategies for their linguistic realisation. This realisation may, however, vary with culture, just as genre conventions may be culture-specific.

While register describes the immediate situational context in which the text is produced referring to the three different areas of text realisation (field, tenor and mode), genre is the overall purpose or function of the interaction. In the words of Martin (1984: 25), a genre is 'a staged, goal-oriented, purposeful activity in which speakers engage as members of our culture'. Less technically, genres may be 'how things get done when language is used to accomplish them'. This leads to the acknowledgement that there are as many genres as there are recognisable activity types in our culture. Some examples are:

- *Literary genres:* poems, short-stories, romantic novels, whodunits, ballads, sonnets, fables, comedies, tragedies, etc.
- *Popular written genres:* instructional manuals, newspaper articles, magazine reports, recipes, etc.
- *Educational genres:* lectures, tutorials, report/essay writing, leading seminars, examinations, text-book writing, etc.
- *Business genres:* business letters, advertisements, brochures and booklets, catalogues, annual reports, meetings, minutes, etc.
- *Legal written genres:* statutes, contracts, deeds, wills, briefs, etc.
- *Other genres:* personal letters, press releases, sermons, obituaries, weather reports, etc.

All cultures have a genre potential, i.e. linguistically-achieved activity types recognised as meaningful in a given culture. Genre potential can be described as the possible configurations of register variables within a given culture at a given time (Eggins, 1994: 26–36). A change of either field, tenor or mode will normally result in a change of genre.

For the translator it is important to be aware of the fact that although the same genres may exist in different cultures, they may in fact be – and often are – structured or composed in different ways. Genre conventions are culture-specific. Thus, for example, the genres 'weather report' and 'death announcement' exist in a Danish as well as in a British context, but they observe quite different conventions in the two cultures.

Currently genre is defined in a number of different ways by different linguists, but in much of the work that has been carried out within a genre-analytic approach, communicative goal or purpose has been used as an important and often primary criterion for deciding whether a particular discourse falls within a particular generic category. An academic article serves to inform, a book review to evaluate, a recipe to instruct, etc.; cf. the following quotation from Swales (1990):

> A genre comprises a class of communicative events, the members of which share some set of communicative purposes. These purposes are recognised by the rationale of the parent discourse community and thereby constitute the rationale for the genre. This rationale shapes the schematic structure of the discourse and influences and constrains choice of content and style. (Swales, 1990: 58)

Within the light of the findings of recent studies in, for example, business genres, the concept of communicative purpose has become more complex, more variable, often multiple, and sometimes hard to get at.

Bhatia's extension of Swales's definition allows for 'private intentions within the framework of socially recognised purposes' (Bhatia, 1993: 13). According to Bhatia (1993: 16), Swales underplays psychological factors and, in that way, undermines the importance of tactical aspects of genre construction, a factor which plays a significant role in the concept of genre as a dynamic social process, as against a static one. Using experienced news reporters as an example, they may be able to insinuate their own preferred political perspectives under the appearance of objective news reports.

In line with this argument, Swales had, in fact, already acknowledged the complexities caused by various kinds of insider knowledge. He points out that while news broadcasts are without doubt designed to keep their audiences up to date with events in the world, they may also have other purposes, such as moulding public opinion, organising public behaviour (as in an emergency), or presenting the controllers and playmaster of the broadcasting organisation in a favourable light (Swales, 1990: 47).

Multiple purposes are evident in the following quotation from Akar and Louhiala-Salminen's (1999) study of faxed business messages:

> In the search of the generic nature of the fax, the content of the English language data was examined in more detail. Using the framework introduced by Swales (1990) and developed by Bhatia (1993), the main purpose of each message was identified, and the 'rhetorical moves' used to achieve the purpose were analysed. Naturally, the general, all encompassing purpose of business messages is to achieve the goals of a buying–selling negotiation, but underneath the 'umbrella' seven sub-purposes could be identified. (Akar & Louhiala-Salminen, 1999: 212–13)

In addition, the spectra of private intentions and strategic manipulation are all too likely to add further 'sets' of communicative purposes and thus further complicate the ascription process. As a consequence, we may no longer be looking at a simple set of communicative purposes, but at a complex layered one. And what is even more important, some of these purposes may not be recognised, at least not officially, by the expert members of the community. Uncovering multiple purposes is thus an important means of understanding a particular genre, and the analysis may even reveal hidden purposes.

1.2 Intra-textual features

An analysis of the situation tells us something significant about how language will be used. While field, tenor and mode (in the narrow sense) describe the speech situation, the text itself unfolds in the following three components: the *ideational function*, the *interpersonal function* and the *textual function* (see also Halliday & Hasan, 1990: 26–7):

FIELD -> THE IDEATIONAL FUNCTION
(language as form and meaning)

TENOR -> THE INTERPERSONAL FUNCTION
(language as communication)
MODE -> THE TEXTUAL FUNCTION
(language as text)

The linguistic features constituting the field of the text are referred to as ideational and/or experiential; those corresponding to tenor as interpersonal; and those to mode as textual. In other words, we imagine a social context and situation in which a set of linguistic features correspond, or put differently, the social context is realised by the linguistic features of field, tenor and mode.

The expression of content, i.e. language as being about something and involving both logical and associational meaning, constitutes the *ideational function*. The speaker's motive in saying something (the communicative function or functional tenor) and the way this is realised in the particular role relationship between sender and receiver (interactional tenor) form the *interpersonal function*.

A further component to be analysed is the linguistic realisation of mode in the *textual function*. The basic distinction is that between speech and writing and the various permutations on such a distinction (e.g. written to be spoken, etc.) generally referred to as the medium. Following Halliday (in his writings as early as 1978: 144–45), mode also includes rhetorical concepts such as expository, didactic, persuasive, descriptive and the like, referred to here as *text-types*. Other aspects included in mode comprise *cohesion* and *thematic organisation*.

1.2.1 The ideational function

The ideational (or experiential) meta-function uses language to encode our experience of the world and to convey a picture of reality whether fictional or non-fictional. We may say that experiential meanings encode our experiences and logical meanings connect those experiences. The ideational meta-function realises the field of the text. When accounting for this function, we are concerned with a number of issues; the taxonomy of the text, participants roles and transitivity, frames and chains evolving from the text, and the way of arranging the message by means of rhetorical strategies (the poetic function). Finally presuppositions, culture-specific elements and intertextuality are dealt with.

(a) Taxonomy: technical/everyday: If field is glossed as the 'topic' of the situation, we need to recognise that a situation may be technical or everyday or somewhere in between these two poles. Eggins (1994) suggests that field varies along a dimension of technicality:

Technical specialised	Everyday common-sense
Technical situation	Everyday situation
assumed knowledge of an activity/institution/area deep taxonomy: detailed sub-classification	common knowledge, no (little) assumed knowledge Shallow taxonomy: limited sub-Classification

Eggins (1994: 71–73) defines taxonomy as lexical relations where one lexical item relates to another through either class/sub-class (rodent/mouse) or part/whole (tail/mouse) relations, i.e. the two classes of hyponomy and *meronymy* (Cruse, 1986; Saeed, 1997). Although most frequently these relations link lexical items which refer to people, places, things and qualities and so are expressed in nominal groups, taxonomic relations can also link processes (verbs, e.g. 'eat – nibble').

Eggins also talks about expectancy relations. These occur where there is a predictable relation between a process (verb) and either the doer of that process, or the one affected by it (e.g. mouse/squeak, nibble/cheese). These relations link nominal elements with verbal elements (see Butt *et al.*, 1995, especially Chapter 3).

(b) Nominalisation: It should be noted that nominalisation is analysed in connection with ideational features because it is often seen to co-occur with a technical choice of lexis. The two following sentences illustrate the process of nominalisation (Eggins, 1994: 57):

> I handed my essay in late because my kids got sick ->
> The reason for the late submission of my essay was the illness of my children.

The first example illustrates language use in everyday situations, the second is an example of specialised language, where the information is said to be 'packed'.

(c) Transitivity: type of verb: The ideational function can typically be explained by answering the question 'Who does what to who under what circumstances?'. The potential *Participants* are realised by nominal groups who revolve around the *Process* (verb) and interact with it through a variety of participant roles, such as agent, goal, etc. The *Circumstances* of human experience covers the whys, whens and wherefores typically realised by adverbial groups and prepositional phrases (see Butt *et al.*, 1995: 42–46).

Type of verb is analysed according to Butt et al.'s interpretation of Halliday's ideas comprising three basic verbal processes: *material, relational* and *projecting*. It is clearly important to a text whether it describes what is happening or being done in the external, material world (material processes), whether it simply describes relationships (relational processes), or if it projects the inner world by speech or thought (projecting processes) (Butt *et al.* 1995: 46). Material processes describe what is happening or being done in the external material world (verbs of doing); relational processes describe relationships (verbs of being); projecting processes project the inner world by speech or thought (verbs of saying or thinking) (see Butt *et al.* 1995: 46–51). It must be noted that rather than thinking of particular verbs as always giving expression to one process type, we should think about how a particular verb is functioning in the context (for exemplification, see Part 2, Section 2.2).

(d) Frames and chains: Realisation of field may be traced in the *frames* and *chains* of the text, which enable us to get an overview of what the text is about. For example, if one receives a postcard about where to register a vote in a local election, the way one understands this information can be described by means of a 'voting-frame'. Thus in 'When you go to the polling station tell the clerk your name and address', the text exhibits a 'voting frame', comprising the 'polling station', 'the clerk', 'your name and address'. Consider also the well-known Clare Russell example (Albrecht, 1998, based on van Dijk, 1980):

> Clare Russell came into the *Clarion* office on the following morning feeling tired and depressed. She went straight to her room, took off her hat, touched her face with a powder puff and sat down at her desk. Her mail was spread out neatly, her blotter was snowy and her inkwell was filled. But she didn't feel like work …

This is the beginning of a crime story expressed in a general 'office-frame' comprising 'Clare Russell', 'the *Clarion* office', 'her room', 'her desk', 'her mail', 'her blotter', 'her inkwell', 'work'. This frame may be further divided into a number of isotopies/chains that fit into the frame: a 'Clare Russell frame' comprising 'tired', 'depressed', 'took off her hat', 'touched her face …', 'sat down', etc.; a specific 'office chain' comprising 'the *Clarion* office', 'desk', 'inkwell', 'mail', 'work'. Such chains may be refined as required to obtain a clear understanding of the text. The frame–chain relationship could be illustrated like this: an office frame, comprising at least two chains: one referring to Clare Russell and one referring to the office and things belonging there:

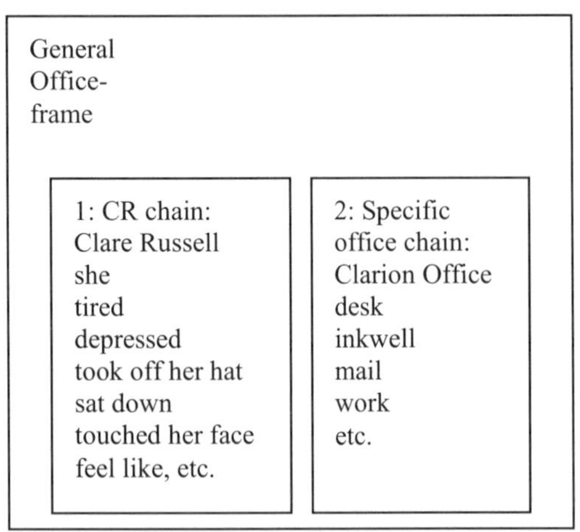

Figure 2 Frame-chain relationships

(e) Collocation: The ideational features of the text may also function as textual features of cohesion in the text. Thus, for instance, a consistent frame creates a systematic whole. Similarly, the phenomenon of *collocation* may be discussed in at least two different ways: (1) as the collocational range of an expression, which is part of what the receiver is told about the field of the text, and (2) as a cohesive feature to be discussed under mode (see Section 1.2.3).

The collocational range of an expression may be defined as the set of contexts in which it can occur (Lyons, 1981: 52). Thus the three words 'flaw', 'defect' and 'blemish' appear to have the same meaning and yet they are not interchangeable. Lyons has pointed out that, whereas it is normal to use either 'blemish' or 'flaw' of someone's complexion and either 'flaw' or 'defect' of someone's argument, it would be odd to use 'blemish' of someone's argument. Knowledge of collocational constraints in the TL is an important aspect of translator competence, just as 'unusual collocations' present a great challenge.

(f) The poetic function: As part of the ideational component, we also consider the poetic function. The following features may be noted: metaphors and unusual collocations, alliterations, parallel structures, balanced sentences, interrupted movement, sound bites. (The concepts of *metaphor* and *image* would require a separate chapter; see, e.g. Lakoff & Johnson, 1980). In addition, repetition, lexical chains, contrast, as well as iconicity are important rhetorical strategies, which additionally contribute to the cohesion of the text.

For exemplification of the features in question, see, for example, an analysis of President Clinton's First Inaugural Address (Trosborg, 2000a).

(g) Presuppositions/culture-specific elements: Each participant in a discourse has a presupposition pool (Brown & Yule, 1983: 79). This pool contains information 'constituted from general knowledge, from the situative context of discourse, and from the completed discourse itself'. For example, discourse subjects might be 'the Queen, John, John's wife', and these elements are in the presupposition pool by virtue of general knowledge, whereas 'your hat, today' are understood from the context of the situation. This pool may be added to as the discourse proceeds.

However, general knowledge in one culture may not necessarily be general knowledge in another. Thus, for instance, *Folketinget* in a Danish text is presupposed as common knowledge, but would have to be explicated somehow in a translation into English such as the *Danish Folketing (Parliament)* or the *Folketing* (Danish Parliament). Folketing cannot be expected to be part of an English speaking person's presupposition pool.

In the presupposition pool, we find cultural as well as professional references that often have to be explained somehow because they cannot be expected to be part of the TT reader's presupposition pool. The point is to identify such elements and to decide on a translation strategy suited to the TT skopos.

(h) Intertextuality: There is a vast number of written texts in the world. To understand any given text or to produce a text we draw on our knowledge of other texts. In identifying what is appropriate in particular discourses and genres, one is automatically appealing to one's knowledge of other texts (Hatim & Mason, 1990: 119). When we 'borrow' from other texts we use intertextual features. If these features are not judged to be part of TT reader's knowledge, explication is needed (cf. the explication of culture-specific references). For an account of intertextuality, see Hatim and Mason (1990), especially Chapter 7.

1.2.2 The interpersonal function

Classifying texts according to fields of discourse amounts to an analysis of lexical-semantic and stylistic features of the chosen subject matter and the specific topic, as outlined in the section on ideational function. In addition, it is desirable to bring together communicative, pragmatic and semiotic values and demonstrate their importance for the development of a text and the way in which communication takes place (cf. Hatim & Mason, 1990: 138). In this connection,

Ferrara (1985: 140) has defined the ultimate goal of text pragmatics as being the study of the entire sequences of speech acts:

> speech acts are evaluated on the basis of higher order expectations about the structure of a text, and how they, being themselves coherent micro-texts, contribute to the global coherence of a larger text. (Quoted in Hatim & Mason, 1990: 139)

In the framework to be presented here, I emphasise the importance of communicative functions. I suggest a twofold distinction of tenor: *interactional tenor* involving sender/receiver constellation (status, expert versus layman, etc.); and *functional tenor* involving communicative functions (realised through speech acts). Hatim and Mason (1990: 51) do, in fact, mention 'a further kind of tenor' in addition to their 'personal tenor', namely 'functional tenor' introduced by Gregory and Carroll (1978: 53) and defined as follows:

> Functional tenor is the category used to describe what language is being used for in the situation. Is the speaker trying to persuade? to exhort? or to discipline?

Hatim and Mason make no further reference to functional tenor, but they do specifiy function as part of tenor in subsequent presentations of text analyses.

Under the label of communicative functions (see later), we compare speech acts as presented by Searle (1969, 1976) and others together with the theory of language functions relating back to Roman Jakobson's 1960 framework.

(a) Communicative functions: Both Austin (1962) and Searle (1969) base their theories on the hypothesis that 'speaking a language is engaging in a rule-governed form of behavior' (Searle, 1969: 11), but whereas Chomsky (1965) conceived of language as a set of sentences, they assume that language can be regarded as a form of verbal acting.

In his article 'A Classification of Illocutionary Acts', Searle (1976: 1ff.) makes a consistent classification of functions of language usage by dividing illocutionary acts into a limited number of major categories. He takes as the chief criterion of classification the speaker's communicative intention manifested in the *illocutionary purpose* (or *point*) of the act (corresponding to the essential condition) and the correspondence between *direction of fit*, i.e. the relation between words and the world, and the psychological state of the mind expressed by the speaker (corresponding to the sincerity condition). He finds that communicative functions are reducible to five major classes, namely *representatives, directives, expressives, commissives* and *declarations*. These categories, in turn, includes subcategories of speech acts.

- *Representatives:* The speaker's purpose in performing representatives is to commit him/herself to the belief that the propositional content of the utterance is true. In an attempt to describe the world, the speaker says how something is, or tries to make 'the words match the world' to use Searle's (1976: 3) expression.
- *Directives:* In performing *directives*, the speaker tries to get the hearer to commit him/herself to some *future* course of action (verbal or non-verbal). As opposed to representatives, directives are attempts to make 'the world

match the words'. *Cost* and *benefit* vary with respect to different illocutionary points; e.g. the purpose of a *request* is to involve the hearer in some future action which has positive consequences for the speaker and may imply costs to the hearer, whereas *a piece of advice* or *a warning* is intended to be in the sole interest of the hearer. In giving *permission* the speaker communicates to the hearer that s/he is not against the hearer carrying out a future action which is in the hearer's own interest and may imply costs to the speaker.

- *Commissives:* In *commissives* the speaker commits him/herself in varying degrees to some future course of action. As was the case with directives, the direction of fit is 'world to words'. In an *offer* the speaker communicates to the hearer that s/he is not against carrying out a future action which is assumed by the speaker to have positive consequences for the hearer, but the speaker is not sure whether the hearer wants this action carried out. A *promise* differs from an offer in that the speaker making a promise has reasons to believe that the hearer is in favour of the speaker carrying out the action in question.
- *Expressives:* The purpose of this class of illocutionary acts is to *express* the speaker's psychological state of mind about or attitude to some prior action or state of affairs. There is no direction of fit, as the intention is neither to describe the world nor to exert an influence on future events; rather, the truth of the propositional content is taken for granted. Expressives vary with regard to propositional content. When *thanking*, the speaker expresses gratitude for the hearer's participation in a prior action which was beneficial to the speaker; in a *complaint* the speaker communicates his/her negative feelings towards the hearer, who is made responsible for a prior action which was against the speaker's interests; an *apology* serves to express regret on the part of the speaker at having performed (or failed to perform) a prior action which had negative consequences for the hearer.
  This category may be further divided into *expressives* and *verdictives*. Expressives are acts which give expression to the speaker's mental and emotional attitude towards a state of affairs (deploring, admiring, etc.), while verdictives are acts which evaluate and relay judgement (assessing, estimating, etc.) (cf. Hatim & Mason, 1990: 60, following Traugott & Pratt, 1980).
- *Declarations:* Declarations require extra-linguistic institutions for their performance; it takes a priest to christen a baby, a dignitary to name a ship, a judge to sentence a defendant, etc. The direction of fit is both 'words to world' and 'world to words', as the actual expression of the declaration brings about a change in reality.

(b) Communicative function (speech acts)/language functions: In outlining the previous functions, Searle has made it clear that he considers language fulfil a *finite* and *determinate* number of functions. A similar view has been adopted by Leech (1983) who, nevertheless, bases his classification of illocutionary functions on different criteria (see Leech, 1983: 104ff.). When comparing these functions to the language functions presented by Roman Jakobson (1960) as in Table 1, the similarities are obvious.

In spite of the overlap, there are, however, some extensions (and omissions) on

Table 1

Searle's categories	*Jakobson's categories*
	Phatic function
Representatives	Informatives
Expressives	Expressives
Directives	Directives
Commissives	
Declarations	
	Metalinguistic function
	Poetic function

both sides. Commissives (acts which commit the speaker to a course of action such as promising, etc. and declarations (acts whose uttering performs the action involved, e.g. 'I baptise you in the name of ...') are not included in Jakobson's model, but he, by contrast, includes *the phatic function, the metalinguistic function* and *the poetic function*. The phatic function is employed to open the channel of communication, to catch the reader's attention, etc. The metalinguistic function addresses the code as such commenting on specific language aspects. In my approach, the metalinguistic function is included in the category of representatives, as metalinguistic utterances are statements, viz. statements about language phenomena. The poetic function, which serves the function of 'decorating' and making the language more interesting to read, is included in the ideational function as a rhetorical device. In conclusion, we are left with the phatic function to be added to Searle's categories, when analysing communicative functions. Finally, it must be mentioned that some theorists (e.g. Traugott & Pratt, 1980) distinguish between expressives and *verdictives*, of which the latter function is used to pass judgement.

Communicative functions and the sub-type of speech act operates at the micro level of analysis, whereas the type at macro level is referred to as *text act*.

(c) Levels of formality: The relationship between sender and addressee is realised in terms of basic distinctions of levels of formality on a scale from formal to informal. Five levels of formality were outlined by Joos in the early 1960s: *frozen, formal, consultative, casual* and *intimate*.

- The *frozen style* is an extreme style that is clearly premeditated, it is marked by social distance between sender and receiver, and it is impersonal. Furthermore, it often makes use of a specific lexicon known only to experts in the particular field. A typical example of a frozen style would be the language used in statutes and contracts.
- A *formal text* would also be well structured, logically sequenced, and strongly coherent. It would be marked for social distance and the syntax would often be impersonal. Typical features are a high frequency of complex sentence structures and noun phrases, absence of contractions; absence of qualifying modal adverbials; absence of subjectivity markers (pronouns, qualifying expressions etc.); diction (lexical items) marked + formal.
- A *consultative text* is written in a neutral 'normal' style. Formal and informal

style markers are absent, receiver participation may be elicited. The diction would involve normal everyday conversational expressions (explicit or implicit) and direct speech may be present.

- A *casual style* would be marked by various degrees of implicitness because of intimacy between sender and receiver. It is used between friends and insiders who have something to share and have shared background information. This style is characterised by simple sentence and noun phrase structure, by ellipsis, and contraction. The diction is informal, colloquial.
- The *final style* is the intimate style used between people who are very close and have a maximum of shared background information.

In order to analyse this parameter, it is crucial to point to simple/complex noun phrases and simple/complex sentences, examine lexis and account for participation.

With regard to participation, it is characterised as simple participation if the sender does not attempt to elicit any responses from the reader of the text. The text is in this sense neutral. Complex participation, on the other hand, does try to elicit some kind of response from the reader, for example by using second-person pronouns, the imperative mood, the interrogative mood or phatic elements:

simple participation:
- phatic elements
- interrogative and imperative structures
response not elicited

complex participation:
+ phatic elements
+ interrogative/imperative structures
+ use of 2nd person pronouns
+ indirect receiver participation
response elicited.

1.2.3 The textual function

The distinction between written and spoken mode (or medium) is an important aspect. Even though the differences between written and spoken language are no doubt familiar, it is important to appreciate that these linguistic differences are the reflex of the situational differences in mode. Compare the situations involving spatial/interpersonal distance and experiential distance resulting in features typical for written language, on the one hand, to the situations lacking distance (spatial/personal or experiential) resulting in features typical of spoken language on the other (see e.g. Eggins, 1994: 55–57). Two respective reference patterns – endophoric reference and exophoric reference – relate to the parameters [+ distance] and [- distance], respectively. In addition to mode, we will consider cohesion, information structure and text-type as part of the textual component.

(a) Cohesion: A central aspect of the textual function is cohesion. The concept of cohesion accounts for the essential semantic relations whereby any passage of speech or writing is enabled to function as text (Halliday & Hasan, 1990: 13). The expression of the semantic unity of the text lies in the cohesion among the

sentences from which it is composed. Each type of text has its own patterns to convey the inter-relationships between persons, objects, and events.

In the words of Baker (1992), who, in turn, draws on Halliday and Hasan (1976) as her primary source, cohesion is defined as follows:

> Cohesion is the network[1] of lexical, grammatical, and other relations which provide links between various parts of a text. These relations or ties organize and, to some extent create text, for instance by requiring the reader to interpret words and expressions by reference to other words and expressions in the surrounding sentences and paragraphs.[2] Cohesion is a surface relation; it connects together the actual words and expressions that we can see or hear ... (Baker, 1992: 180)
>
> Note 1 is to the effect that Baker uses 'network' in its non-technical sense and not as a systemic term. Note 2 explains that cohesion does exist within sentences but what is significant is intersentence cohesion.

In their well-established framework, Halliday and Hasan identify five cohesive devices in English: *reference, substitution, ellipsis, conjunction* and *lexical cohesion*, of which only reference (reiteration) and lexical cohesion (collocation) are discussed here.

Reference as a cohesive device: Reiteration depends on repetition of lexical items but does not necessarily involve the identity of the referent. Traditionally, the word reference is used in semantics for the relationship which holds between a word and what it points to in the real world (for example 'table' referring to a particular table being identified on a particular occasion). In Halliday and Hasan's model of cohesion, reference is used in a more restricted sense: reference is limited to the identity relationship which holds between two linguistic expressions, instead of denoting a direct relationship between words and extra-linguistic objects. Cohesion lies in the continuity of reference. Where the interpretation of any item in the discourse requires making reference to some other item in the discourse, there is cohesion. Thus, a reference item has the potential of directing the reader/hearer to look elsewhere for its interpretation. One element is interpreted by reference to another (Halliday & Hasan, 1990: 11), and reference is a device that allows the reader/hearer to trace participants, entities, events, etc. in a text (Baker, 1992: 181).

In addition to the restricted notion of reference based on textual rather than extra-linguistic relations, Halliday and Hasan also acknowledge that the reference relationship may be established situationally. They distinguish between *textual endophora*: referring to a thing as identified in the surrounding text, and *situational exophora*, referring to a thing as identified in the context of situation. Textual endophora can be to preceding text (anaphora) or to following text (cataphora), whereas exophoric reference denotes an extra-linguistic relationship (Halliday & Hasan, 1990: 32–33). Note that exophoric references as such are not cohesive in that they point towards 'participants' in the situational context.

Referential categories: Halliday and Hasan outline five reference categories which constitute a continuum of cohesive elements that may be used to refer back to an entity already mentioned in the discourse. This continuum stretches from full repetition at one end of the scale to pronominal reference at the other, as shown in the following example adapted from Halliday and Hasan (1976: 283) and quoted in Baker (1992: 183):

> There's a boy climbing that tree.
> (a) The boy is going to fall if he doesn't take care. (repetition)
> (b) The lad's going to fall if he doesn't take care. (synonym)
> (c) The child is going to fall if he doesn't take care. (superordinate)
> (d) The idiot's going to fall if he doesn't take care. (general word)
> (e) He's going to fall if he doesn't take care. (pronominal reference)

Note that all five examples include a pronominal reference (*he* used with anaphoric reference to the category being discussed).

A further means of reference is co-reference, typical of, for example, journalism. The following chain of co-referential items is adopted from Baker (1992: 182): Mrs Thatcher – The Prime Minister -> The Iron Lady -> Maggie. If a line is drawn between what is linguistic or textual and what is extra-linguistic or situational, co-reference is not strictly a linguistic feature, but a matter of world knowledge.

Pronominal reference: One of the most common patterns of establishing chains of reference in English and a number of other languages is to mention a participant explicitly, for example by name and title, and then use a pronoun to refer back to the same participant in the immediate context. Third-person pronouns are frequently used with anaphoric reference to an entity that has already been introduced in the discourse. On encountering a pronoun, the reader will automatically look to the surrounding text for its referent. Pronominal reference comprises personal reference, comparative reference and a third category of demonstrative reference.

Personal reference: The category of personals includes three classes: personal pronouns, possessive determiners, and possessive pronouns (Halliday & Hasan, 1990: 43) as exemplified in the following sentences *I have a book, It is my book, The book is mine.* As Halliday and Hasan (1990: 45) point out, the term 'person' might seem a bit misleading, because the system includes not only reference to persons but also non-personal objects. The technical term is not part of any linguistic theory; it is simply an 'address' for easy recovery.

Personals referring to the speech roles (speaker and addressee) are typically exophoric: this includes *I* and *you*, and *we* meaning *I* and *you*. They do, however, become anaphoric in quoted speech and so are normally anaphoric in many varieties of written language. Personals referring to other roles (persons or objects other than the speaker or addressee) are typically anaphoric; this includes *he, she, it* and *they*, and also the 'third-person' component of we when present (Halliday & Hasan, 1990: 50ff).

As has been pointed out, it is only the anaphoric type of reference that is relevant to cohesion, since only that type provides a link with a preceding portion of the text. When we talk of the cohesive function of personal reference, it is, therefore, particularly the third-person forms we have in mind.

Comparative reference: The notion of 'general comparison' refers to comparison in terms of likeness and unlikeness, without respect to any particular property: two things may be the same, similar or different (where 'different' includes both 'not the same' and 'not similar'). In contrast, 'particular comparison' refers to comparison that is in respect of quantity and quality (*more/fewer/less, better/equally good*; Halliday & Hasan, 1990: 77–8).

General comparison expresses likeness between things. The likeness may take the form of identity, where two things are, in fact, the same thing (there is identity), or of similarity, where two things are like each other (there is non-identity but likeness).

> It's the same cat as the one we saw yesterday (identity)
> It's a similar cat to the one we saw yesterday (similarity)
> It's a different cat from the one we saw yesterday (non-identity, non-similarity?)

Demonstrative reference: Demonstrative reference is a form of verbal pointing (see : 81–82). The members of the system indicate a scale of proximity (nearness). Here the is neutral. It merely indicates that the item in question is specific and that somewhere the information necessary to identify it can be found. *This, these, here* and *now* refer to something 'near', whereas *that, those, there* and *then* refer to something 'far'. A few examples will illustrate the difference as well as the cohesive function (Albrecht, 1995):

> There seems to have been a great deal of carelessness.
> This is what I can't understand.

> There seems to have been a great deal of carelessness.
> Yes, that's what I can't understand.

> We're going to the opera tonight. This'll be our first outing for months.
> We went to the opera last night. That was our first outing for months.

Collocation: Whereas reiteration depends on repetition of lexical items, collocation covers a pair of (or several) associated items in a text, such as:

> Various kinds of oppositeness of meaning, e.g. 'boy/girl', 'employer/employee', 'buy/sell', 'landlord/tenant', 'lease/rent', etc.
> Associations between pairs of words from the same ordered series, e.g. 'Monday/Friday', 'January/August', 'pound/shilling/pence', etc.
> Associations between pairs of words from unordered lexical sets, e.g.
> - part–whole relations: 'car/brake', 'contract/paragraph'
> - part–part relations: 'eye/mouth/chin', 'recitals/definitions'
> - co-hyponomy: 'blue/yellow/green' (colour), 'statute/contract/deed' (legal documents).

Lexical cohesion typically operates through lexical chains throughout a text to create a unified whole. Several cohesive chains may operate in the same text.

As mentioned, substitution, ellipsis and conjunction are also important cohesive devices. For lack of space, these devices are not discussed here, but some examples are given in Part 2, Section 4.2. In addition, cohesion may be achieved by a variety of other devices, such as structure, consistency of style, continuity of tense, and punctuation devices such as colons and semicolons.

(b) Thematic structure: We use textual meanings to organise our experiential and interpersonal meanings into a linear and coherent whole. Throughout a text, the writer makes use of signposts to guide the reader from beginning to end. In

this section, we are concerned with how to structure information within the clause in terms of *theme/rheme organisation* and how to build up texts by the progression of themes.

In English (and a number of other languages as well), what comes first expresses an important and separate kind of meaning: *the theme*. The primary requirement of theme is to signal the point of departure for the experience of the clause. Following Butt *et al.* 1995: 91–95), we distinguish between *topical, interpersonal* and *textual themes*.

The *topical theme* gives the point of departure for the experiential meaning involving participant, process, and circumstances by giving emphasis to the element that has been chosen to start the clause:

> *Peter* bought a new jacket at Harrods.
> *A new jacket* was bought at Harrods.
> At *Harrods*, Peter bought a new jacket.

The highlighted elements are the themes, i.e. what the sender has chosen to focus on, while the rest is the rheme, i.e. what the sender has chosen to say about the theme. The sender can either stay with a theme, or bring different elements in or out of psychological focus. A typical way of developing a topic is theme/rheme progression, in which the rheme of one sentence develops into the theme of the following sentence (see Part 2, section 4.3. for examples).

Interpersonal themes indicate interaction between writers and their readers and the positions that are taken. The most common is interrogative clauses, where the interpersonal theme is the finite verb in polar questions or the *wh*-element as unmarked subject:

> *May* we have your order at your first convenience?
> *When* can we expect to receive your order?

To signal the writer's position or standpoint, adverbials are typical:

> *Hopefully*, we can have your order by Monday.

We talk about textual theme, if the experiential meaning is prefaced with a group or phrase which functions to connect our message to the previous text. By means of this device, we can create a cohesive text in which the connections between messages are well signposted. Conjunctions are most likely to occur in the beginning of clauses, and, when they do, they must be considered thematic. It is often possible to tell something about the purpose of a text by examining its textual themes. For example, *if, although, unless, because, in order to*, etc. are likely to introduce clauses which enhance the argument.

If the clause has only topical themes, be it participant, process or circumstance, the theme is *simple*. If the theme has been divided into topical, textual and interpersonal themes, the clause is said to have *multiple themes*.

For further analysis of thematic structure, see Butt *et al.* (1995: Ch. 6). For actual textual examples, see Section 4.3 in Part II.

(c) Text types: The classification of texts into rhetorical modes are named text-types. The text type of a text is defined as *narrative, descriptive, expository, argumentative* or *instrumental*. This is in agreement with the framework presented

by Hatim and Mason (1990). For characteristics of each type, see Hatim and Mason (1990) and Albrecht (1995). Text-type operates at the micro level of analysis, whereas the type at macro level is referred to as the *contextual focus* or text-type focus.

Texts can be seen as the bringing together of mutually relevant communicative intentions. Text-type is referred to as 'a conceptual framework which enables us to classify texts in terms of communicative intentions serving an overall rhetorical purpose' (Hatim & Mason, 1990: 140), and rhetorical purpose is understood in the sense of a set of mutually relevant communicative intentions. In this way we are able to combine the analysis of communicative functions and text type and set up expectations: for example, an expository text is supposed to involve a high number of representatives, whereas expressives are allowed (and expected) in argumentative texts.

The distinction between genre and text type is an important one, as genre values are often confused with what I refer to as text types. Researchers will refer to the expository genre, the argumentative genre, or even the appellative genre. Martin (1992), for example, would split the genres into descriptive, expository and narrative texts, the communicative purpose is thus to describe, explain and narrate, and not the purpose of, for example, an entire brochure as such. However, a genre as, for example, a leader in a newspaper would quite often involve more than one text type, often expository as well as argumentative types, but would still be only one genre – a leader. I suggest that we keep the notion of genre (the generic value) as reserved for whole texts, whereas text types (the rhetorical values) are properties of individual texts.

(d) Genre versus medium: Technological advances affect the way in which genre exemplars are perceived and ranked in relation to their mode of transmission: telex, fax, phone, e-mail, face-to-face meeting, videoconference, on-line journal, print journal and so on. Is e-business the biggest thing since the industrial revolution, or is the Internet just another useful tool for speeding up business communications, a bit like a telephone?

Take, for example, the website. Are websites genres? Websites bring together exponents of a lot of previously independent genres (company brochures, product descriptions, etc.) and allow them to interact with each other, so that they could be exponents of a super-genre, if there were such a thing. Even if diachronically this super-genre was an anthology, synchronically it could be a new type. However, a wiser way of looking at it is to consider the website to be a medium, on the level with the newspaper or television channel: it allows genres to exist.

However, we can observe the birth of a new genre in the homepage. The homepage is not a derived genre, but rather what we may call a 'daughter genre' and its ancestors are the table of contents, the advert, the physical reception desk and the front page of a periodical.

A new media may result in the adaptation of old genres. For exemplification, Greg Myers (2000) accounts for the changes in lectures due to new technological advances (power-point). This forms a contrast to the actual rise of new genres caused by new media such as the homepage and the 'chat' on internet, or FAQ (frequently asked questions) on the net.

To sum up this point, new media may give rise to new genres as well as modify already existing ones. The big unknowable is how a completely networked world will change the way in which people work with each other.

Part 2: A Sample Textual Analysis

In this second part, I will illustrate the analytical approach on the basis of an example. The sample text is entitled 'Not Quite Across the Rubicon'; it was published in the weekly publication *The Economist* on 27 February 1999.

2.1. Situational features

2.1.1 Place of communication

The place of communication is Great Britain, and the text is written exclusively in unmarked standard British English. This can be seen from British English expressions such as 'odd', 'Tory' and 'bobbed up', which in American English would have been 'weird/strange', 'Conservative' and 'showed up'. Mixtures of British and American English do not occur.

2.1.2 Time of communication

The time of communication is also unmarked as contemporary, the date of publishing being 27 February 1999. The text does, however, contain a few archaic terms such as 'Rubicon' and 'Machiavellian''

2.1.3 Social class

Social class is also unmarked, as no social (or regional) dialects are found. The text is intended for the educated middle-class. The occurrence of terms/people such as 'Rubicon', 'Leonid Brezhnev', 'Supreme Soviet', 'Kremlinologists', 'Machiavellian', etc. means that the reader is expected to be both educated and interested not only in British politics but also to a certain degree in Russian politics and must have quite a degree of background knowledge on the subject. This classification of the reader goes well with the average reader of *The Economist*, which is thought to be from the educated middle-class and interested in politics, economy, etc.

2.1.4 Purpose of communication

The author's intention with the text is to analyse and comment on the Prime Minister Tony Blair's recent pro-euro speech in the House of Commons and give his opinion about and reasons for the Prime Minister's former and present strategies and actions. In the article the author tries to analyse Tony Blair's intentions and motives for the speech and adds his own opinion in various ways.

2.1.5 Register

(a) Field: The domain of the text is politics as can be seen from the various references to ministers, the referendum, the euro, etc. (cf. Section 2.2.4 on lexical chains), the subject matter is Tony Blair's pro-euro speech in the House of Commons, and the topics in the text focus on such aspects as why Tony Blair's speech was so cryptic that he seems to have turned pro-euro, how the press handles the situation, how he prepares himself and his government for the referendum and who his opponents are.

The page layout is quite simple: it displays three main constituents – headline, text and illustration – and the immediate message communicated to the reader is direct and very clear. This directness and clarity is initially achieved by means of an illustration, which is placed in the very centre of the page as the obvious focus of attention. The illustration is surrounded by the actual column text and on top of everything the headline 'Not Quite Across the Rubicon' is placed. This headline establishes a direct link to the situation depicted in the illustration and in this connection it should be noted that the centre part of the page does not merely display an illustration: It is in fact a caricature (and a very humorous one, indeed) which portrays Tony Blair playing the part of Julius Caesar crossing the river Rubicon with the devoted assistance of two British Conservatives (Michael Heseltine and Kenneth Clarke). By including this expressive illustration the text succeeds in providing the reader with direct and immediately comprehensible links to the actual contents of the text. Thus it becomes clear to the reader that the main character of the text is Tony Blair, that British Conservative politicians occupy the minor roles, and that a parallel may be drawn between the situation which is to be discussed in the text and the expression 'crossing the Rubicon' – to take a final and decisive step towards something. However, the added wording in the text 'not quite' in the headline indicates that in this particular case the decisive step has not yet been taken.

(b) Tenor: The first category here is *sender*: the sender of the text is the British international weekly magazine *The Economist*, which is a magazine that discusses current world affairs from a financial angle and goes much more into details than the daily newspapers. *The Economist has regular columns concerning the USA, Asia, Britain, Business*, etc. *The Economist* generally enjoys a good reputation as it is regarded as a serious magazine, which deals with and discusses current affairs from around the world in well-documented articles and columns. As indicated by its title, *The Economist* primarily discusses its selected topics from a financial angle and thus the most obvious circle of readers of the magazine comprises business people or people who have a particular interest in the financial and/or political world. A remarkable feature of *The Economist* and its style of writing is the fact that every single article and column in the magazine is written anonymously. *The Economist* speaks with a collective voice and the main reason for this deliberate anonymity is a belief that what is written is more important than who writes it. The editorial focus is placed on the actual message of communication – the messenger is deemed irrelevant. Like most other modern news covering media, *The Economist* offers its readers a constant up-date via its Internet home page.

A recurrent feature of *The Economist* is its short columns under the headline *Bagehot*, which are often written and/or illustrated with a humorous and ironic 'twist'. The headline *Bagehot* refers to *Walter Bagehot*, the most famous editor of *The Economist* (from 1861–1877), who is best remembered for his political writing and for his firm belief in plain language. Thus Mr Bagehot strove to be 'conversational, to put things in the most direct and picturesque manner, as people would talk to each other in common speech, to remember and use expressive colloquialisms' (as stated on *The Economist* website, cf. (www.economist.com), and by naming this recurrent column after him, it seems that The Economist seeks to uphold the conventions introduced by Mr Bagehot.

The next category is *receiver*: The receiver of the text is whoever reads *The Economist*. However, this requires an identification of the average reader once again:

the average reader would typically be educated middle-class, well-informed business people with a particular interest in politics and economy. The people who buy and subscribe to *The Economist* are probably people who already read one or several newspapers but wish to be informed in detail about certain subjects. This particular article aims at people interested in British and EU politics. This can be seen in the fact that political concepts are not explained, so the reader is expected to have quite some background knowledge.

Sender/receiver relationship: The author may be assumed to be a regular writer in the Bagehot column and, as such, to have extensive knowledge of both national and international politics. S/he seems to be a semi-expert on especially British politics as s/he displays impressive knowledge about Blair, his strategies, motives, supporters, opponents, etc. Hence the relationship could be described as somewhat asymmetrical. The author has inside knowledge and can explain in detail what the reader knows only in broad outline.

(c) Mode: The genre – established as a super-ordinate category – has already been defined as a leader. Typical of leaders is the written mode, which generally stays within one category: written to be read, as is the case in this article.

2.2 Ideational features of language

This section is the linguistic realisation of field. It will focus on the ideational functions of language in the text taking as its starting point the taxonomy of the text. It will then account for transitivity (process types and participants), semantic aspects, such as frames/chains, metaphors and images, intertextuality and culture-specific elements. Apart from metaphors, the poetic function is not paid particular attention to, even though instances of, for example, parallel structures, balanced sentences and alliteration do occur.

2.2.1 The taxonomy of the text

The taxonomy of the text is mostly shallow (i.e. with few sub-categories), but there are a few cases of deep taxonomy: speech -> formulation -> arrangements -> job; plan -> programme -> arrangements -> job. The text is mainly written in everyday language, though with the occurrence of some formal features: 'at first glance', 'thereupon', 'for the present'. Examples of everyday expressions are 'Tory', 'dull' and 'bobbed up'. As examples of technical language can be mentioned 'Supreme Soviet', 'Kremlinologists', 'Hansard', etc. As there are no explanations for these terms they heighten the formality/style of the text and limit the audience to people who know what the author is talking about.

Normally, the shallower the taxonomy the less background the reader is supposed to have in order to understand the text. However, in this case, even though the taxonomy is shallow, the reader does need quite some background knowledge to fully understand the text.

Nominalisations are typical in technical texts and generally make texts more difficult to read. There are only a few nominalisations in the text, e.g. 'Germany's mounting demands for a reduction of Britain's EU budget rebate'.

2.2.2 Transitivity

When considering transitivity, we need to look at the participant–process–participant structure.

(a) Verbal processes: The verbal processes of the text may be divided in three main

categories: *material, relational* and *projecting*. The text displays a number of relational and projecting processes. The vast majority of processes, however, belong to the category of material processes. These processes are used to denote and describe actions and actual physical activities within the text (emphasis added:

> The prime minister stands up in the House of Commons …
> and by flashing them out early …
> … all the Tories' better-known pro-Europeans (…) tottered to their feet …
> Mr Heseltine even bobbed up later on television …

These verbal processes add to the dynamics of the text: They make the text seem more dynamic by referring to the sequence of events in a value-laden manner using words and expressions which may be characterised as colloquial language. The active style is further emphasised by the fact that the text does not display an extensive use of nominalisations or the passive voice. On the contrary, it seems that a more active and congruent style is preferred. Another striking feature, which particularly concerns the three last-mentioned examples, is the strong visual, and in many cases, also humorous appeal, which is conveyed by applying a metaphorical and figurative angle to the verbal processes. Thus the reader may actually be able to visualise the Tories fumblingly tottering to their feet to congratulate the Prime Minister on his new plan. Just as the image of Michael Heseltine bobbing up on the television screen is very likely to make at least some readers smile.

The relational processes – in this text mostly realised by various forms of the verb 'be' – mainly describe personal qualities and attributes relating to the participants of the text:

> … that he *is* in favour of taking Britain into the euro …
> … as if Tony Blair *were* some Leonid Brezhnev …
> Mr. Blair *is* usually cautious.
> He *was*, therefore, sensibly careful in 1997 …
> … to remind Mr. Blair that he *was* available …

Note that the relational process quoted in the second example expresses a hypothetical verbal process in the form of a metaphor.

The projecting verbal processes of the text are primarily related to expressions of knowledge and/or opinion and in many cases these processes are used to denote utterances which establish the interpersonal relationship between the participants of the text:

> … the *Sun* duly *denounced* him for having decided by stealth …
> … *The Times inveighed* solemnly against the danger …
> Mr Hague (…) *accused* the prime minister of throwing away …
> … Paddy Ashdown *congratulated* the prime minister on at last crossing …

Thus by using value-laden projecting verbs, the text cleverly and quite elegantly succeeds in implicitly commenting on aspects of the interpersonal relations existing between the participants without directly referring to these relations.

(b) Participants: The participants of the text are realised by nominal groups which are mainly related to concrete elements within the text. These concrete

participants may refer to persons, places, specific events, and to the names of political parties and newspapers. The vast majority of these participants is realised by fairly simple nominal groups: 'the prime minister', 'the House of Commons', 'the euro', 'the referendum', 'the Liberal Democrats', etc.

A remarkable feature relating to the textual participants is the extensive use of 'name-dropping' throughout the text. The names of politicians and newspapers are mentioned repeatedly; thereby the factuality of the text is underlined and the reader's attention is drawn to the main participants within the textual framework.

2.2.3 Circumstances

The circumstances of the text are almost exclusively realised by adverbial groups and prepositional phrases. These circumstances may be divided into three major categories relating to specific areas within the text. One group of circumstances is related to the temporal aspects of the text, another is primarily concerned with defining the various locations within the text. The third category – which is indeed the most interesting one – is the category in which the writer very elegantly 'peeps' out and almost conspicuously becomes an active commentator of the processes and participants of the text:

> 'perfectly good' -> the writer comments on the previous strategy of the PM
> 'sensibly' -> the writer comments on the value of decisions and actions of the PM
> 'duly' -> the writer rather ironically comments on the attitudes of another newspaper
> 'solemnly' -> another ironic evaluation of a second newspaper
> 'eccentrically' -> a third newspaper is commented on with a slight sense of irony
> 'pretty well' -> positive evaluation of the PM's performance in the Commons.

By means of very delicate instruments expressed solely via simple and often single-word adverbials, the writer succeeds in making a very clear and evaluative statement relating to the participants of the text.

2.2.4 Lexical frames/chains

Lexical frames and chains create coherence throughout the text and emphasise, through the use of certain words, the topics of the text. The participants of this text may easily be traced in the textual *frames*. These frames fall into three categories, which combine into an overall pattern and function as the topical 'skeleton' of the text. The first frame is related to the purely economic aspects of the text:

(1) *Economy/the euro:* the euro; Europe's new currency; economic tests; change-over plan; single currency; monetary union; the single-currency plunge; euro-battles; debates on the euro; economic conditions; stagnant, unreformed economies; EU budget rebate; europhiles; euro-sceptical; the beloved pound; pro-euro; euro membership; pro-Europeans.

This frame comprises all the participants that are directly linked to the overall topic of the text. When moving further into the framework of the text, the next two frames reveal themselves:

(2) *Politics:* prime minister; the House of Commons; Gordon Brown; chancellor; Tony Blair; Leonid Brezhnev; the Supreme Soviet; spin-intensive administration; Kremlinologist; government; Hansard; Mr. Blair; referendum; the Conservative party; William Hague; election; parliamentary performance; Mr. Hague; self-determination; the Commons; the Conservative's; the Tory cause; ballot; party members; voted; parliaments; Parliament; the Tories' better-known pro-Europeans; pro-euro Tories; British voters, Edward Heath, Kenneth Clarke; Michael Heseltine, campaign, the Liberal Democrats; Paddy Ashdown.
(3) *Media/public:* newspapers; the media; public opinion; British opinion; the Murdoch press; *The Sun*; the people's wishes; *The Times*; the *Daily Telegraph*; angry headlines; hostile headlines; horrid headlines; the euro-sceptical press; television.

These frames, which include the participants relating to politics on the one side and the media and public on the other side, discuss and comment on the first frame. Thus, the participants relating to the last two frames are the actors of the text, whereas the first frame represents the more passive participants – those discussed by the active frames.

Chains have to do with more specific things, for example 'Secrets' – hidden meaning; cryptic speech; between the lines; never appear; unveil – and 'Tony Blair's character' – good hedging strategy; cautious; fateful decision; rubs against the grain; sensibly in no hurry; promised; sensibly careful; not tie his hands; enjoyed the sensation. The author shifts between the chains in order to help the reader stay on track and create certain connotations, just as these chains help the reader define the author's point of view.

2.2.5 Metaphors and images

A very striking feature of the text is its clever use of expressive metaphors. The author makes use of metaphors/images to make the text seem more interesting and vivid. This makes a politically oriented text like 'Not Quite Across the Rubicon', which could easily have been very dull, come alive and thereby keep the reader interested. Of overall importance is the structuring metaphor concerning the Rubicon. The very first elements catching the reader's eye are the caricature and the headline which combine into the overall structural metaphor of the text: Tony Blair as Julius Caesar about to 'cross the Rubicon'/about to enter Britain into the euro. However, this Rubicon metaphor does not only function as an eye-catching extra-textual element: The metaphor has also been entered into the intra-textual element of the text where it runs like a red thread through the text. Reference is made to the 11 EU states which took the 'single-currency plunge' and 'have remained afloat'. By choosing these particular verbs, which have a clear connotative link to the water/river element, the writer deliberately pursues the extra-textually established metaphor. This deliberate metaphorical pursuit can also be traced later in the text: the expression 'flushing them out' is used to explain the strategic choices of the prime minister in relation to the handling of his political opponents. The metaphor is carried through to the very end of the text – the very last line mentions the prime minister's 'testing the water' – a clear-cut reference to the overall structural metaphor of the text.

Another metaphorical element is displayed in a hypothetical simile-like construction comparing Tony Blair to the former Soviet Union leader Leonid Brezhnev: 'as if Tony Blair were some Leonid Brezhnev uttering a cryptic speech in front of the Supreme Soviet'. In this metaphorical element, objects from two different domains, British politics and Soviet Union politics, are explicitly compared and this makes the text expressive and visually appealing to the reader. Other examples are: 'train newspapers' (as if newspapers were animals); 'move closer to monetary union' (as if it were a place you could move to); '[h]is previous position struck this column' (a position hardly strikes anything); 'flushing them out' (as if there were a giant toilet you could use to flush out meaning. The author also creates the image of 'a dress rehearsal' of 'the fight he will have on his hands', when he does come to call a referendum.

2.2.6 Intertextuality and culture-specific references

Both instances of intertexuality and culture-specific references are exophoric references, i.e. references outside the text. The interpretation of both requires presupposed knowledge: in the case of the former, knowledge of another text to which reference has alrady been made is required; in the case of the latter the reference is specific to the source culture (or some other culture) and interpretation is dependent on knowledge of the particular culture. Finally, the interpretation of textual references may require presupposed knowledge of a more general kind (e.g. world knowledge, international politics) or of a more specific kind (e.g. expertise or technical knowledge).

There are a number of examples of intertextuality in the text requiring background knowledge of the reader in order to understand fully the text. An example is the headline: 'Not Quite Across the Rubicon', which refers to a river named Rubicon that separated Italy from Cisaepine Gaul, the province allotted to Julius Caesar. By leading an army across this river, contrary to the prohibition of the civil government at Rome, Caesar precipitated the civil war, which resulted in the death of Pompeii and the overthrow of the senate. Hence, the phrase 'to cross the Rubicon' signifies taking the decisive step by which one is committed to hazardous enterprise from which there is no retreat.

The text is very culture-bound, which means that it contains many culture-specific elements that are intended for the source-culture reader. For instance, in the beginning of the text, it is not spelt out who the Prime Minister is, or what the House of Commons refers to. Only later do we encounter the name of Tony Blair, still not linked up with his title as Prime Minister. Other culture-specific elements are the various British newspapers, the number of politicians mentioned in the text, and 'the Hansard' – all of which require specific knowledge of the British political system. There are also culture-specific references that refer to a culture outside the British one, namely references to Russian culture: 'Leonid Brezhnev', 'Supreme Soviet', 'Kremlinologist', etc. The interpretation of 'a spin-intensive administration' also requires specific knowledge, although this may be said to presuppose political knowledge (of spin-doctors) rather than culture-specific knowledge. Thus the writer makes use of culture-specific references and political terminology in an international magazine whose readers are supposed to be well informed about global themes and political matters.

2.3. Interpersonal features of language

In this section, the emphasis is on *communicative functions* expressing the intentions of the writer and on *level of formality* realising the degree of formality/intimacy by means of which the message is conveyed according to the relationship between sender and receiver.

2.3.1 Communicative functions

The author would like to give the impression that he is describing a factual state of affairs. He uses a Representative style by asking questions and answering them. However, when examining the text closely, it is obvious that the dominant communicative function used in the text is the expressive function. The focus of attention is on the sender, and the choice of words is subjective and personal. This can already be seen in the first line of the text 'At first glance it is odd'. The reason why it is odd is solely because the author thinks so and is trying to force a certain attitude onto the reader.

The writer's attitude is revealed mainly in his choice of lexis. A negative attitude is conveyed by many adjectives and adverbials: 'perfectly plainly'; 'loyal chancellor'; 'portentous title'; 'dull; 'ineffable fashion'; negative comparison to communism – most western European people think of communism as something negative. Further negative connotations are seen in 'train animals', 'sounded silly', 'decided by stealth'. Compare also the many adverbials mentioned as circumstances in Section 2.2.3 above: 'perfectly good'; 'sensibly'; 'duly'; 'solemnly'; 'eccentrically'; 'pretty well'). These negative connotations are used to guide the reader's mind towards negativity so as to relate the actual topics with negative aspects (as mentioned in connection with the newspapers). '[T]he wrath of the Murdoch press' is a connotative link to Steinbeck's novel *The Grapes of Wrath*. Positive connotations are evident in expressions such as 'perfectly good', 'familiarity', 'in favour of and 'enjoyed the sensation' used in connection with Blair.

An author may use both epistemic and deontic modality. The first one is used to express degree of likelihood, the second one to express the degree of desirability. In this text, there is a number of modals expressing possibility, e.g. the occurrence of 'can', 'may', 'will', 'would' and 'could' as *hedges*; either the author is not fully committed to the truth value of his/her statements, or s/he refers to other sources, e.g. he (Blair) 'must have known'; 'may have made it harder'. Thus the use of epistemic modality functions as *shields* for the author to hide behind, and makes what would otherwise have been representatives appear as tentative statements.

Deontic modality is not used in the text, neither do we find instances of imperatives. Apart from two rhetorical questions, the mood is exclusively declarative. This indicates lack of directives and, as could be expected, the author is not trying to influence the reader to do something, though he may want the reader to adopt his or her opinion. The use of rhetorical questions call for the reader's active considerations and expressions of attitude: 'So why was the prime minister's announcement thereupon poured over for hidden meaning, as if Tony Blair were some Leonid Brezhnev uttering a cryptic speech in front of the Supreme Soviet?'; 'Why, then, did Mr Blair take trouble this week to stir things up?' Note the use of the subjunctive in the first question. The use of the interrogative mood is closely linked to the instances of complex participation reflected by the text: the use of the second person pronoun *you* in the text indicates that the sender seeks to elicit some kind of response from the reader. Thus by including direct questions and directly appealing to the reader's personal participation, the author succeeds in adding even more elements to the textual dynamics and expressiveness.

We may argue that the rhetorical questions have a phatic function. The following structures exemplify characteristic speech acts in the text:

(1) *Representatives* (with expressive elements highlighted):
- The prime minister stands up in the House of Commons and says, *perfectly plainly*, that he is in favour of taking Britain into the euro ...
- *The Times* inveighed *solemnly* against the danger of British convergence with the '*stagnant, unreformed economics*' of the European mainland
- Mr Hague, in a parliamentary performance which the *Daily Telegraph* judged eccentrically to be his best to date ...

(2) *Expressives*:
- Mr Blair is usually *cautious*
- There were a lot of *horrid* headlines

(3) *Verdictives*:
- ... the government's national changeover plan, which behind its *portentous title is a dull programme of technical arrangement* ...
- *That goes too far:* Blair has left himself *plenty of room* to stay out of the euro if he decides he cannot win a referendum.
- *At the most*, he has *tested the water*.

2.3.2 Level of formality

When considering the level of formality, we need to pay attention to the structure of the text, the choice of lexis, the grammatical complexity as well the degree of interaction with the reader. It is crucial to point to simple/complex NPs and simple/complex sentences, examine lexis and account for participation.

In general, the text bears the marks of a well-structured text: the thematic progression of the text and its textual elements are logically sequenced. As mentioned in Section 2.2.5, the metaphorical framework of the text functions as a structuring element. This particular feature is strong evidence that the text has indeed been carefully structured and planned in advance, which in turn is indicative of a high degree of formality.

However, the majority of the syntactic characteristics of the text are not those of a formal text. The author seems to prefer a congruent style to a more packed style, which would for instance have included a high frequency of complex noun phrases, nominalisations and abstract participants. Furthermore, the text displays several value judgements (cf. the many expressives and verdictives), it includes subjectivity markers and asks questions which are directly aimed at the reader. By contrast, examples of syntactic complexity are also evident, for example:

> More damaging still to the Tory cause was the squashing of any hope that last summer's ballot of party members, in which they voted overwhelmingly to stay out of the euro for at least two parliaments, would silence the pro-euro Tories in Parliament.

Note also complex noun phrases such as 'Germany's mounting demands for a reduction of Britain's EU budget rebate'.

The attitude in lexis revealed by the text further substantiates the ambiguous characterisation of the level of formality. The text uses everyday conversational expressions, such as 'pretty well', and even colloquial style, e.g. 'bobbed up'. This style is cleverly mixed with expressions which are characteristic of very formal and literary language, e.g. 'portentous'; 'ineffable'; 'the wrath of the Murdoch press'; 'prosper'. This creates a very personal and rather sophisticated style.

2.4. The textual function

Exploring the textual function involves the logical organisation of the ideational and the interpersonal meanings of the text. The analysis will include a determination of *text type* and examinations of *cohesive elements* in the text. Furthermore, the *information structure* of the text will be briefly commented on.

2.4.1 Text type

The text does not make use of only one text type. On the contrary, it is a mixture of exposition including narrative passages and argumentation. The text displays several features relating to *conceptual exposition*. This text may well be defined as writing that explains: It begins with a detailed outline and organisation of the overall subject matter of the text, namely the presentation of Tony Blair's announcement in the House of Commons in the first paragraph. This presentation provides the reader with the relevant background information relating to the textual topic and it denotes the point of departure from where the text will develop. Furthermore, the text directly poses questions relating to the textual topic and these questions are subsequently discussed and explained by the text itself:

> So why was the prime minister's announcement thereupon pored over for hidden meaning...? -> Because the prime minister ...

The trouble is that the author answers his questions in a subjective manner (cf. the many expressives identified in Section 2.3.1). The subjective undertone is already evident in the first line of the text: 'AT FIRST glance it is odd', 'odd' in the opinion of the author. Thus the text starts with a *tone setter*, it is a statement that sets the scene in a subjective manner and is anticipatory of a text which aims at managing or steering the reader's conception. In contrast, an expository text would generally start with a *scene setter*, which is a topic sentence intended to set the scene in a neutral way, thus anticipating a text which monitors rather than manipulates the reader. Even when the author is narrating events, his attitude shines through:

> After the prime minister's statement, all the Tories' better-known pro-Europeans – Edward Heath, Kenneth Clarke and Michael Heseltine – tottered to their feet ...

The mixture of narration, exposition and argumentation, often with argumentation as the *contextual focus* is characteristic of leaders and editorials, and this article is no exception.

2.4.2 Cohesion

Cohesion is concerned with the way in which the author links sentences and passages of a text. It can be divided into grammatical, lexico-grammatical and lexical cohesion. Grammatical cohesion within the text is mainly accomplished by means of anaphoric references. These references may be demonstrative as indicated by the first example or they may be personal as indicated by the second example:

> the lips of the prime minister those of his loyal chancellor
> Mr Blair is usually cautious <-he knows that ...

Furthermore, the text includes examples of verbal substitution and nominal ellipsis:

> ... that Mr Blair *had made a mistake* <-Except that he seldom does
> all the Tories better-known pro-Europeans <- some/none

Lexico-grammatical cohesion is realised by the use of conjunctions combining grammatical and lexical features. The conjunctions express the internal relations between sentences of the text, which may be additive ('and'); adversative ('except', 'but', 'though'); causal ('therefore', 'because') and temporal ('for the present', 'by then', 'on the morning afterwards', etc.). Some examples are given below:

Adversative conjunctions:

- But because it was he and not the chancellor who presented the plan ...
- But the fulminations of the euro-sceptical press ...

Causal conjunctions:

- So why was the prime minister's announcement ... pored over for hidden meaning ...?
- Because the prime minister wanted it that way.
- He was, therefore, sensibly in no hurry ...

In addition, the text displays features of strong lexical cohesion. The lexical ties are accomplished by the use of metaphorical elements which have already been analysed. By deliberately applying the extra-textually established Rubicon metaphor to the intra-extual environment, the text succeeds in creating strong *metaphorical cohesion. In addition to this, the text established several chains of lexical collocation*. These chains include lexical items which are connected by clear lexico-semantic relations and which are also co-references:

> 'the euro' – 'Europe's new currency' – 'the single currency'
> 'pro-euro' – 'pro-Europeans' – 'europhiles'
> 'the prime minister' – 'Tony Blair' – 'Mr Blair' – 'he'/'his'.

Finally, it may be noted that *reiterations* realised by consistent 'name-dropping' throughout the text also serve as a cohesive feature within the intra-textual framework.

2.4.3 Thematic organisation

(a) *Topical themes*: The normal unmarked progression of the topic is subject – verb (complement) - adverbial. This is also true of this text 'The prime minister stands up in the House of Commons ...', but a considerable number of marked themes are found.

A marked theme occurs when an element other than the subject is moved to the front of a sentence in order to topicalise this element. Typical is the topicalisation of adverbials and of complements; for example:

> '*At first glance* it is odd ...' means that at second glance it is not odd.
> 'Formally, all Mr *Blair was doing this week* ...' places focus on 'formally' and 'all'.
> '*On the morning after, the Sun* ...' focuses on the quick reaction of the press.
> '*As for the commons*, the rehearsal went pretty well ...' to build up coherence.
> *More damaging still to the Tory cause* was the squashing of any hope ...' focuses on the damage.
> '*None* was cowed by their own leader's official policy of scepticism ...' marked due to the passive construction.
> '*For the liberal democrats*, Paddy Ashdown ...' focuses on the party, not the person.

Marked themes are to be kept in the translation in order to keep the focus as intended by the ST author.

(b) Interpersonal and textual themes: When analysing the theme structure of the text, it appears that the sender interacts with the readers by means of questions. The presence of mood adjuncts such as 'better still'; 'perhaps'; 'more probably'; 'at the most'; 'perhaps even' shows that the sender is present in the text and that he is being subjective. When the conjunction appears at the beginning of a sentence (as it usually does), the conjunction is an instance of textual theme signalling to the receiver how this sentence is to be related to the preceding one. As it appears under lexico-grammatical cohesion (Section 2.4.2), this text has a number of conjunctions pointing to causes and contrasts, which is typical of argumentative texts.

(c) Theme/rheme progression: The analysis shows that the focus is on Tony Blair as he occupies the topical part of 'theme'. Another aspect of the structure is to determine whether the text is coherent, which can be done by looking at the thematic progression. In this text, the theme–rheme structure is dominant, which means that the sender does not re-use rhemes as themes, but sticks to the themes already introduced. This, however, does not mean that the text lacks cohesion because this has been achieved lexically, most often by 'he', 'Tony Blair' and 'Prime Minister'. Choosing a prevailing theme in the text is a consequence of Blair being the predominant topic, while theme/rheme progression would indicate progression of one topic into the next.

Instead of repeating a theme thus enlarging upon this theme adding new information, themes in a text may change. An obvious way of progression is to let the rheme of one structure appear as theme, as can be seen in the following examples:

You (theme) might almost think, surveying the angry headlines, that *Mr Blair* had made a mistake (rheme)
Except that *he* (theme) seldom does (rheme)

He (theme) knows that *leading Britain into the euro could be the most fateful decision he will ever take* (rheme)
It (theme) is also the one big issue ... (rheme)

A theme may be repeated in full or in part as in the examples below:

After the prime minister's statement, *all the Tories' better-known pro-Europeans* ...
Some said *they* wished ...
None was cowed by *their* own leader's official policy ...
Mr Heseltine even bobbed up later on television ...

Examples of partitive repetition of theme as rhemes occur for example when the structure 'He (Blair) must have known that this would arouse the instant wrath of the Murdoch press, and points beyond...' is followed by statements by the various newspapers: 'The *Sun* duly denounced ...'; '*The Times* inveighed solemnly ...'; 'Mr Hague, in a parliamentary performance which the *Daily Telegraph* judged eccentrically ...'.

Part 3: Translation

In this part, I will discuss consequences of a detailed ST analysis for translation. At first, some relevant concepts of Translation Studies will be introduced, and then the strategies for translating this text into Danish will be commented on on the basis of the framework provided.

3.1 Theories of translation

The field of Translation Studies (TS) has undergone a number of changes. As an interdisciplinary discipline, it has been influenced by a number of fields: linguistics and psycholinguistics, recent development in text linguistics and discourse analysis, and not least by trends in social anthropology and the ethnography of speaking with the growing number of cross-cultural studies resulting from these developments. It has changed from a preoccupation with literature to a concern with general language and specialised language; from limited text types and rigid equivalence types to holistic gestalt-like principles; from a concern with isolated words to text-in-situation with emphasis on cultural background. A text is no longer seen as a static specimen of language but as a verbalised expression of an author's intention; translation is not seen as a mere transcoding process but as a cross-cultural event. Interpretation is not supposed to take place from the micro level of the word ('bottom-up' processing) but from the macro structure of the text to the micro unit of the word ('top-down' processing). Orientation towards the function of the target text (prospective translation) prevails prescriptions concerning the TT by relating it to the ST (retrospective translation), and translations are regarded as concrete assignments serving specific functions (not as model translations).

Translation quality assessment is thus no longer based exclusively on the criterion of equivalence (as required by House, 1976). For one thing, equivalence may not be possible because of diverging linguistic systems in SL and TL. For another, equivalence may not even be a desirable criterion. Here we present the two major models: *the equivalence model* and the *skopos theory*.

3.1.1 The equivalence model

The equivalence model involves various types as they were introduced by various TS scholars. I will only list the most frequently used concepts, without engaging in a more substantial debate.

Equivalence types were set up, for example the following:

- *totale Äquivalenz* (total equivalence);
- *fakultative Äquivalenz* (facultative equivalence, i.e. one to many equivalence), e.g.: German: *Spannung*; English: voltage, tension, suspense, stress, pressure;
- *approximate Äquivalenz* (approximative equivalence, i.e. one-to-part-of-one correspondence), e.g. German/Danish: *Himmel/himmel*; English: *heaven, sky (cf. Kade, 1968);*
- *formal versus dynamic equivalence* (see Nida, 1964), with dynamic equivalence meaning the closest natural equivalent, e.g. 'The Lamb of God' -> 'The Seal of God' (in the Eskimo culture);
- *Structural equivalence*
  equivalence at text level (Filipec, 1971)
  'textbound equivalence' (Neubert, 1984);
- Pragmatic equivalence.

Similar types are used by Baker (1992) in her book *In Other Words, cf. the chapter headings: 1 Equivalence at word level; 2 Equivalence above word level; 3 Grammatical equivalence; 5 Textual equivalence: thematic and information structures; 5 Textual equivalence: cohesion; 6 Pragmatic equivalence.*

With respect to texts in different languages, it has been argued that they can be equivalent

- in *different degrees* (fully or partially equivalent);
- in respect of *different levels* of presentation (equivalent in respect of context, of semantics, of grammar, of lexis, etc.);
- at *different ranks* (word-for-word, phrase-for-phrase, sentence-for-sentence).

However, the demand for equivalence has been heavily criticised by, among others, Snell-Hornby, cf.

> Äquivalenz – as a narrow, purpose-specific and rigorously scientific constant – has become increasingly static and one-dimensional, equivalence (leaving aside the TG-influenced concepts of the 1960s) has become increasingly approximative and vague to the point of complete insignificance. (Snell-Hornby, 1988: 21)

> As a fundamental principle we may say that the simplest interlingual relationship – where the term equivalence is still justified – exists at the level of terminology and nomenclature, though even here reservations are called for. (Snell-Hornby, 1988: 106)

In the present model, the *skopos theory* as devised by Nord (1997) is used. Her major distinction between *documentary* and *instrumental* translation, each with a number of sub-categories is seen as superior to previous notions such as literal vs. free, semantic versus communicative, SC-oriented versus TC-oriented, etc.

3.1.2 Skopos theory

Skopos theory is part of 'a general theory of translation' which was first presented by Vermeer in 1978. *Skopos* is Greek and means *aim, target, purpose*. The theory hinges on the so-called 'skopos rule' with its sociological sub-rule: 'Human interaction (and as its subcategory: translation) is determined by its purpose (skopos), and therefore it is a function of its purpose ...' (Nord, 1991: 24).

According to the skopos theory (Nord,1991: 8), a translation must fulfil certain requirements, which are defined by the 'translation instructions' (translation assignments), in order to be suitable for a certain purpose. These instructions, which must consist of a more or less explicit description of the prospective target situation are referred to as the 'skopos', i.e. the text function of the TT.

The notion of *text function* means the communicative function, or the combination of communicative functions, which a text fulfils in its concrete situation of production/reception. It is derived from the specific configuration of extra-textual factors comprising *sender/sender's role, intention, recipient/recipient's expectation, medium, place, time* and *motive* (Nord, 1991: 70). Translation is seen as 'the production of a functional target text maintaining a relationship with a given source text that is specified according to the intended or demanded function of the target text (translation skopos)', and allows 'a communicative act to take place which because of existing linguistic and cultural barriers would not have been possible without it' (Nord, 1991: 28).

The function of the TT is not arrived at automatically from an analysis of the ST, but it must be pragmatically defined by the purpose of the TT (Nord,1991: 9). Furthermore, as every TT recipient will be different from the ST recipient in at least one respect – s/he is a member of another cultural and linguistic community – functional equivalence between ST and TT is not the 'normal' skopos of a translation, but an exceptional case in which the factor 'change of functions' is assigned zero (Nord, 1991: 23). According to this view, the initial task of the translator is to compare the (prospective) function-in-culture of the TT required by the initiator with the 'function-in-culture' of the ST in order to identify those ST elements which have to be preserved or adapted in the translation. In a functional view of translation, equivalence between ST and TT is regarded as being subordinate to all possible translation scopes and not as a translation principle that is valid 'once and for all' (cf. Reiss & Vermeer, 1984: 146ff.).

The target recipient has a different knowledge of the world, a different way of life, a different perspective on things, and a different 'text experience' in the light of which the TT is read (Nord, 1991: 24). It follows that the target reader handles the text in a different way, maybe s/he is not familiar with the subject matter, or he/she needs to be 'filled in' on ST specific cultural phenomena. To meet this demand, the feature of 'adaptation' must be part of the concept of translation as a strategy which demands particular attention on the translator's part. The translator becomes the central figure in the process of intercultural communication, but the translator must always adhere to the principle of loyalty, which has two directions: towards the ST, and towards the TT reader .

The broader notion of function (the 'skopos' of the text) is crucial. Rather than adhering to the rigid dichotomy of specialised and non-specialised text as being decisive for determining the desired degree of equivalence, it is the translator's task to consider the relevant dimensions for each individual text or type of text. A crucial distinction has been made between *documentary translation* and *instrumental translation*. The TT can be seen as

(a) 'a document of a past communicative action in which the source culture sender made an offer of information to a source culture recipient by means of a ST',
(b) 'an instrument in a new target culture communicative action, in which the target culture recipient receives an offer of information for which the ST served as a kind of model'. (Nord, 1991: 72)

Thus, a documentary translation serves as a document of a source culture communication between the author and the ST recipient reproducing certain aspects of the ST or the whole ST-in-situation for the TT recipient, who is conscious of 'observing' a communicative situation of which s/he is not part. An instrumental translation, by contrast, is a communicative instrument in its own right, which can focus on some features of the ST, while pushing others into the background (cf. Nord, 1991: 72–3).

The following sub-categories have been defined by Nord:

Documentary translation	*Instrumental translation*
Interlinear version	Equifunctional translation
Literal translation	Heterofunctional translation
Philological translation	Homologous translation
Exoticising translation	

The categories of documentary translation are all seen as having a metatextual function, whereas the categories of instrumental translation either preserve or change communicative functions (phatic, referential, expressive, directive). For further explication and exemplification, see Nord (1997).

Although the distinction between say 'semantic' and 'communicative' (Newmark, 1981) may appear to be similar to the notions of 'documentary' and 'instrumental', the two approaches are widely different in their focus. First and foremost because the starting point of skopos theory is different. What is decisive for the choice of translation strategy is the skopos (the purpose of the translation). This is in sharp contrast to previous models, where the ST was the ultimate determiner. Note also that an instrumental translation allows for an equifunctional translation.

In conclusion, a strict polarised dichotomy must be abandoned in favour of a target-oriented approach taking into consideration translation as an instance of communication embedded within a given situation, and viewed within a broader sociocultural context. The validity/suitability of Nord's sub-categories are open to discussion, but beyond the scope of this paper.

When adapting a translation, it is crucial to distinguish between changes necessitated by diverging linguistic systems, on the one hand, and changes determined by the function of the TT in agreement with the 'translation instructions' (cf. the translation skopos) received by the translator, on the other. In other words, a distinction must be made between adaptations forced on the translator through linguistic/cultural differences between the SL and culture and target language and culture over which the translator has no control, and adaptations which result from intentional choices made by the translator in order to comply with purposes and intentions outlined in the given translation instructions. Cultural phenomena have a special status and are thus particularly problematic for the translator; source-culture-specific phenomena may have to be either preserved or 'implanted' in the target culture, dependent on the type of text and on the purpose of the translation.

Finally, it must be emphasised that the translator is responsible for his/her partners in the translation interaction. The concept of 'loyalty' has been stressed by Nord (1997: 47–8). When adapting a text this must be done with due respect to the concept of loyalty which commits the translator bilaterally to the source and the target side. It is the translator's task to 'mediate' between the two cultures without falling into the trap of 'cultural imperialism', i.e. without pretending that the concept of culture A is superior and, therefore, must be adopted by others.

3.2 Translation strategies for 'Not Quite Across the Rubicon'

In order to arrive at an adequate translation strategy, the ST skopos – i.e. the function in situation of the ST – has to be compared to the TT skopos. Allowing for changes, we need to know exactly which aspects are to be adapted and which are to remain unchanged. It should then be possible to decide on the specific translation strategy/ies, and the requirements for adaptation can be spelled out and complied with. Note that in this approach it is of the utmost importance for the translator to know the TT skopos of the translation. This must be presented to students in their assignments in order to secure translation tasks close to the demands of real life. Knowing the purpose of a translation is therefore an indispensable demand.

In the following we establish major parameters in ST and TT profiles:

(a) Source text profile:

Time/Place:	Great Britain 1999
Field:	The main field is British politics
Subject matter:	Tony Blair's announcement of being in favour of joining the euro
Tenor:	
Sender:	*The Economist*
Receiver:	Well-educated middle class people interested in British politics
Sender-receiver relationship:	The social role is somewhat symmetrical, as there are no explanations and much information is presupposed, intertextual references. The sender must be regarded as a semi-expert possessing political insight.
Mode:	The genre is a leader from *The Economist*.

	Purpose:	The evaluation of Tony Blair's announcement of being in favour of joining the euro and the reaction hereof, which imply that Britain has taken an important step towards joining the euro. *The Economist* seeks to convince the readers that the final step has not yet been taken.
(b)	*TT profile*	
	Time/Place:	Denmark 1999
	Field:	As source text
	Subject matter:	As source text
	Tenor:	
	Sender:	The Danish newspaper *Politiken*
	Receiver:	Danish educated middle-class people reading *Politiken*.
	Sender-receiver relationship:	The social role is asymmetrical as the TT receivers' know-ledge of British politics is not as detailed as that of the ST receivers. Thus the culture-specific elements and the inter-textual references need to be explained.
	Mode:	The genre is an article.
	Purpose:	The purpose of bringing the translated version of 'Not Quite Across the Rubicon' in *Politiken* is to inform the Danish readers of Britain's stance on joining the euro as a contribution to the discussion as to whether Denmark should join or not.

When deciding on a specific translation strategy, we note that the ST profile and the TT profile are similar. What has been changed is place and readership and with that a slight change of purpose. As mentioned previously, the readers of *Politiken* are less advanced on matters of British politics. The Danish readers cannot be assumed to possess the relevant background knowledge on political and cultural aspects and, therefore, the social role relationship is now asymmetrical. With regard to purpose, the text that is required is to give an account of Prime Minister Blair's attitude to the euro as perceived by *The Economist* before the Danish referendum on the same matter.

One could opt for a documentary translation for the purpose of documenting the opinion of *The Economist*. However, it is not a text strictly documenting the wording of *The Economist*, although the magazine is the ultimate source demanding the translator's loyalty, just as the journal must be explicitly mentioned as the source. But it must also be kept in mind that the article in *The Economist* is aimed at a global readership, even though the section in which it appears is concerned particularly with British affairs. We therefore opt for an equifunctional instrumental translation, in which the text is adapted particularly to the Danish readership. The major 'adjustment' lies in producing a translation that meets the demands of the TT skopos which differs slightly from that of the ST.

The textual analysis provides a guide to the translator both as regards the many aspects to be preserved and as regards changes. An in-depth analysis was undertaken to enable the translator to know clearly what is conveyed by the text. Rendering the structure and meaning of the English text as accurately as possible in agreement with the ST analysis for aspects to be preserved is in itself a major task for the translator. However, here the translation comments are mainly concerned with elements that need to be changed in order to adapt the text for Danish readers and the slight change of purpose. The aspects in need of adaptation are culture-specific elements, intertextual references and other presuppositions, i.e. instances where the gap in the TT readers' knowledge pool is to be compensated for when relevant to the understanding of the translation. I will not comment here on problems that are specific to translation into the Danish language.

The ST has been analysed in detail to give the translator a clear understanding of the major linguistic, textual and sociocultural aspects. The analysis of the extra-textual as well as the intra-textual features of the text has revealed many elements within the text and its framework that deserve the translator's special attention.

In broad terms, the aspects under the ideational function is to be preserved as far as technicality, transitivity and semantic aspects (including frames) are concerned. Preserving the meaning of the metaphorical structure in the ST presents a challenge of its own, but though desirable, this aim cannot be fully achieved. First of all, the structural Rubicon metaphor gives rise to translation difficulties. The translation should necessarily reflect a similar structuring metaphorical element. However, when considering the TT audience, the readers of the Danish daily newspaper *Politiken*, which has been defined as a rather broad non-specialist audience, it is likely that directly transferring the Rubicon metaphor would be asking too much of the TT audience. This belief is supported by the fact that information on the Rubicon metaphor is not to be found in contemporary encyclopaedias in Danish. On the basis of these considerations, it is suggested that we change the metaphorical element so instead of using the 'crossing the Rubicon' expression, the expression 'the die is cast' (*alea iacta est*) is used as a structuring metaphorical element. This expression is not only commonly known in Denmark, it also has clear connotative links to Caesar's irrevocable decision at the Rubicon. Note that this metaphorical substitution leaves the caricature included in the ST rather meaningless: one would have to leave out the illustration, or have another cartoon made by *Politiken's* caricaturist.

Adjustments of collocations/idiomatic expressions must be carried out to bring these expressions into accordance with modern standard Danish. Thus in the statement: 'except that the words issued this time from the lips of the prime minister' must leave out 'lips' or substitute 'mouth' for 'lips' in order to be idiomatically correct in Danish.

In the following statement: 'One of the advantages of running a spin-intensive administration is that you can train newspapers to think like Kremlinologists' would demand an explanation of the expressions 'spin-intensive' and 'Kremlinologists' in order to be accessible to the defined Danish readership.

Finally, most of the aspects mentioned in Section 2.2.6 as intertextual and culture-specific elements and presuppositions would require additional explanations when translating the text for a Danish audience. In connection with the names of British politicians and newspapers, adaptations may include explanatory appositions stated in direct relation to the names. Thus 'British' has to be added when translating 'Prime Minister', 'Chancellor' and 'Government'. However, in relation to the expressions 'Hansard', 'the Murdoch press' and 'Machiavellian', the most obvious choice would be to replace these specific expressions by broader and more generally perceptive expressions. Thus, the translation of 'Hansard' would, for instance, only include a general reference to the official summaries of parliamentary debates in any country – without stating the exact name 'Hansard' .

With regard to the *interpersonal function*, communicative functions including the persuasive tone are to be preserved. It must be admitted, though, that the persuasive element of the ST loses some of its direct appeal, as the attempt to influence primary readers is somewhat lost in relation to secondary readers (the readers of the translation), even though the translation is brought as an element to be considered in the Danish debate before the referendum on the Danish membership of the euro.

Caused by a change in sender/receiver relationship, the level of formality is to be lowered. This implies that complex lexical items are to be explained or substituted by more general terms, just as very complex noun phrases and sentences will have to be broken up in order to meet the Danish ideal conventions of reader-friendliness, which is required as the Danish readers of *Politiken* are not necessarily used to reading complex linguistic structures. A noun phrase such as 'Germany's mounting demands for a reduction of Britain's EU budget rebate', and a complex sentence as 'More damaging still to the Tory cause was the squashing of any hope that last summer's ballot of party members, in which they voted overwhelmingly to stay out of the euro for at least two parliaments, would silence the pro-euro Tories in Parliament' would have to be split up to ease reading.

With regard to the *textual function*, the argumentative style is to be preserved. The translation must be internally coherent and, as a general rule, the thematic focus and the theme/rheme structure of the ST is to be transferred to the TT.

Finally, it must be emphasised that the ultimate guide to carrying out this translation task, namely an in-depth ST text analysis, must be complied with as accurately and appropriately as possible, even though these aspects have not been given particular attention in this part on translation.

This approach to textual analysis, as presented here, is used in a course on 'Textual Analysis and Translation' for advanced students at the Aarhus School of Business. Students are presented with the model as outlined in the Appendix, and they are encouraged to apply it to any text they are translating. They translate a text, and together with the TT, they are expected to submit a written comment showing how they worked through the categories as listed on the guidelines presented in the Appendix. They are requested to give a brief explanation of the categories used, to comment on and draw conclusions on their analysis as they go along, and to summarise the findings for outlining the translation strategy. They are requested to avoid simple long lists, but instead provide convincing explanations.

Concluding Comments

This paper has been concerned with approaches to translation, in particular the equivalence and the skopos models. The ST analysis of a particular text has been undertaken in order to create a deep understanding of the text. The TT skopos has been defined and compared to that of the ST in order to be able to specify which aspects need to be preserved and which have to be adapted for the TT receivers. The aspects in need of adaptation have been pointed out, while at the same time the importance of rendering as accurately as possible those aspects which do not undergo adaptations has been stressed.

It could be argued that the presented textual analysis describes a 'bottom-up' process for arriving at a thorough understanding of the ST. However, a 'bottom-up' process is not recommended for the translation task as such; on the contrary, the very purpose of the skopos approach is to work 'top-down' with the TT functions as outlined in the TT profile as decisive criteria when treating the aspects outlined in the ideational, the interpersonal and the textual components.

The drawbacks of a 'bottom-up' approach are many when it comes to translating: Students may be tempted to keep as closely as possible to ST structures, which is likely to lead to linguistic interferences and mistakes even when translating into the native language; they also run the risk of losing sight of the text as a whole, just as differences in cultural orientation may easily be neglected. Thus, translation should not become a code-switching operation with emphasis on lexical and syntactical equivalences, i.e. with the focus of attention directed towards smaller units of language. Instead, the perspective of seeing the text as a whole within its communicative situation and cultural orientation has been emphasised.

Today, the extent to which a text is translatable is thought to vary with the degree to which it is embedded in its own specific culture, and with the distance that separates the cultural background of ST and TT audience in terms of time, place, etc. (the 'scale of translatability'). We should not expect theoretical models of translation to solve all the problems a translator encounters. Instead, theories should formulate a set of strategies for approaching problems and for coordinating the different aspects entailed. Finally, even though translation theory is now prospering, and great efforts are invested in translator training, translations as products may never be perfect. Even when an experienced translator 'completes' his/her 'final' version, a tiny insistent voice may still be saying: 'Hang on a minute; I've got a great idea!' (cf. Bell, 1991: 75).

References

Akar, D. and Louhiala-Salminen, L. (1999) Towards a new genre: A comparative study of faxes. In F. Bargiela-Chiappini and C. Nickerson (eds) *Writing Business: Genres, Media and Discourses* (pp. 207–226). Harlow: Longman.

Albrecht, L. (1995) *Textual Analysis.* Copenhagen: Sam fundslitteratur.

Albrecht, L. (1998) Key model for textual analysis for translation purposes. Unpublished lecture notes, The Aarhus School of Business.

Austin, J.L. (1962) *How to Do Things With Words.* New York: Oxford University Press.

Baker, M. (1992) *In Other Words. A Course-book on Translation.* London/New York: Routledge.

Bell, R.T. (1991) *Trannslation and Translating: Theory and Practice.* London: Longman.

Bhatia, V.K. (1993) *Analysing Genre. Language Use in Professional Settings.* London/New York: Longman.

Brown, G. and Yule, G. (1983) *Discourse Analysis.* Cambridge: Cambridge University Press.

Butt, D., Fahey, R., Sprinks, S. and Yallop, C. (1995) *Using Functional Grammar. An Explorer's Guide.* Macquarie University: National Centre for English Language Teaching and Research.

Chomsky, N. (1965) *Aspects of the Theory of Syntax.* Cambridge, MA: MIT Press.

Cruse, D.A. (1968) *Lexical Semantics*. Cambridge: Cambridge University Press.
Eggins, S. (1994) *An Introduction to Systemic Functional Linguistics*. London: Pinter.
Ferrara, A. (1985) An extended theory of speech acts: Appropriateness conditions for subordinate acts in sequences. *Journal of Pragmatics* 4, 233–252.
Filipec, J. (1971) Der Äquivalenzbegriff und das Problem der Übersetzbarkeit. *Zeitschrift Fremdsprachen* V/VI, 81–85.
Firth, J.R. (1951) *Papers in Linguistics: 1934–1951*. Oxford: Oxford University Press.
Gregory, M. and Carroll, S. (1978) *Language and Situation: Language Varieties and their Social Contexts*. London: Routledge & Kegan Paul.
Halliday, M.A.K. (1978) *Language as Social Semiotic: The Social Interpretation of Language and Meaning*. London: Edward Arnold.
Halliday, M.A.K. and Hasan, R. (1976) *Cohesion in English*. London: Longman.
Halliday, M.A.K. and Hasan, R. (1990) *Cohesion in English* (10th edn). London: Longman.
Halliday, M.A.K., McIntosh, A. and Strevens, P. (1964) *The Linguistic Sciences and Language Teaching*. London: Longman.
Hatim, B. and Mason, I. (1990) *Discourse and the Translator*. London/New York: Longman.
House, J. (1976) *A Model for Translation Quality Assessment*. Tübingen: Narr.
House, J. (1981) *A Model for Translation Quality Assessment* (2nd edn). Tübingen: Narr.
Hymes, D. (1971) *On Communicative Competence*. Philadelphia: University of Pennsylvania Press.
Jakobson, R. (1960) Linguistics and poetics. In T.A. Sebeok (ed.) *Style in Language* (pp. 350–77). Cambridge, MA: M.I.T. Press.
Joos, M. (1969) *The Five Clocks*. New York: Harcourt Brace.
Kade, O. (1968) *Zufall und Gesetzmäßigkeit in der ÜbersetzungO (Beiheft I zur Zeitschrift Fremdsprachen)*. Leipzig: Enzyklopädie.
Lakoff, G. and Johnson, M. (1980) *Metaphors We Live By*. Chicago: University of Chicago Press.
Leech, G.N. (1983) *Principles of Pragmatics*. London/New York: Longman.
Lyons, J. (1981) *Language and Linguistics: An Introduction*. Cambridge: Cambridge University Press.
Malinowsky, B. (1923) The problem of meaning in primitive languages. Supplement 1 to C.K. Ogden and I.A. Richards (eds) *The Meaning of Meaning*. London: Kegan Paul.
Martin, J.R. (1984) Language, register and genre. In F. Christie (ed.) *Children Writing: Reader* (pp. 21–29). Geelong, Vic: Deakin University Press.
Martin, J.R. (1985) Process and text: Two aspects of human semiosis. In J.D. Benson and W.S. Greaves (eds) *Systemic Perspectives on Discourse* (Vol. 1, pp. 248–74). Norwood, NJ: Ablex.
Martin, J.R. (1992) *English System and Structures*. Amsterdam: Benjamins.
Myers, G. (2000) Powerpoints, technology, lecture and changing genres. In A. Trosborg (ed.) *Analysing Professional Genres* (pp. 177–93). Amsterdam and Philadelphia: Benjamins.
Neubert, A. (1984) Text-bound translation teaching. In W. Wilss and G. Thome (eds) *Translation Theory and its Implementation in the Teaching of Translating and Intyerpreting* (pp. 61–70). Tübingen: Narr.
Newmark, P. (1981) *Approaches to Translation*. Oxford: Pergamon.
Nida, E.A. (1964) *Towards a Science of Translating. With Special Reference to Principles and Procedures Involved in Bible Translating*. Leiden: Brill.
Nord, C. (1991) *Text Analysis in Translation*. Amsterdam/Atlanta: Rodopi.
Nord, C. (1997) A functional typology of translations. In A. Trosborg (ed.) *Text Typology and Translation* (pp. 43–67). Amsterdam and Philadelphia: Benjamins.
Ogden, C.K. and Richards, I.A. (1923) *The Meaning of Meaning*. London: Kegan Paul.
Reiss, K. and Vermeer, H.J. (1984) *Grundlegung einer allgemeinen Translationstheorie*. Tübingen: Niemeyer.
Saeed, J.I. (1997) *Semantics*. Oxford: Blackwell Publishers.
Searle, J.R. (1969) *Speech Acts*. Cambridge: Cambridge University Press.
Searle, J.R. (1976) The classification of illocutionary acts. *Language in Society* 5, 1–24.
Snell-Hornby, M. (1988) *Translation Studies. An Integrated Approach*. Amsterdam and Philadelphia: Benjamins.

Swales, J.M. (1990) *Genre Analysis. English in Academic and Research Settings*. Cambridge: Cambridge University Press.
Traugott, E.C. and Pratt, M.L. (1980) *Linguistics for Students of Literature*. New York: Harcout Brace Jovanovitch.
Trosborg, A. (ed.) (1997) *Text Typology and Translation*. Amsterdam and Philadelphia: Benjamins.
Trosborg, A. (2000a) The inaugural address. In A. Trosborg (ed.) *Analysing Professional Genres* (pp. 121–47). Amsterdam and Philadelphia: Benjamins.
Trosborg, A. (ed.) (2000b) *Analysing Professional Genres*. Amsterdam and Philadelphia: Benjamins.
van Dijk, Teun A. (1980) *Text and Context. Explorations in the Semantics and Pragmatics of Discourse*. London: Longman.
Vermeer, H.J. (1978) Ein Rahmen für eine allgemeine Translationstheorie. *Lebende Sprachen* 23, 99–102.

Appendix: Textual Analysis and Translation

A. Translation-oriented text analysis of source text

(1 extra-textual features; 2–4 intra-textual features

1. Situational aspects

Place of communication
  unmarked – standard AmE/BrE
  marked – regional dialects
Time of communication
  unmarked – contemporary
  marked – e.g. archaic items
Social class
  unmarked – educated middle class – standard language
  marked – other social dialects
Purpose of communication

Field: domain, subject matter, topic(s), short outline of text
Tenor: sender – receiver
  sender/receiver relationship
  social role – symmetrical (solidarity, equality)
        – asymmetrical (authority – impersonal)

Mode: medium of communication

  simple medium: language style stays within one category
  e.g. spoken to be heard, written to be read

  complex medium: language does not stay within one category
  e.g. written text to be spoken as if not written, written text to be read as if heard

Genre

2. Ideational/experiential features of language (realisation of field – language as meaning)

Taxonomy: technical/everyday

  describe syntax: e.g. nominalisation, type of verb
  describe lexis

Semantic aspects incl. frames, unusual collocations, metaphors, images, etc.

The poetic function: parallel structures, balanced constructions, interrupted movements, alliterations, rhymes, etc.

Intertextuality, exophoric references, culture-specific elements
(needs a translation comment, for example under Gricean maxims)

3. Interpersonal features of language
(realisation of tenor – language as communication)

Communicative functions, speech acts
representatives (incl. metalinguistic statements)
expressives, verdictives, directives and declarations
as marked by mood in verbs, modal verbs, attitude in lexis, etc.
politeness

Level of formality – frozen, formal, consultative, casual, intimate
point to simple/complex NPs and simple/complex noun phrases

simple participation:
– phatic elements
– interrogative and imperative structures,
response not elicited

complex participation:
+ phatic elements
+interrogative/imperative structures
+use of 2nd person pronouns
+ indirect receiver participation
response elicited

4. Textual features of language
(realisation of mode – language as text)

Cohesion
grammatical cohesion: endophoric references (anaphoric references – cataphoric references), substitution, ellipsis
lexical cohesion: reiteration (repetition, co-reference) and collocations at text level (iconic linkage)

Information structure – focus, given/new

Text type (narration, description, exposition, argumentation, instruction), text-type focus

B. SPECIFICATION of ST SKOPOS and TT SKOPOS

C. TRANSLATION STRATEGY (incl. Gricean maxims)

D. TRANSLATION, TRANSLATION COMMENTS

Debate

Text and Genre Analysis for Translators: Structure, Content and Function of the Model

Christina Schäffner (Aston University): Before we look at the structure of the model, it might be useful to explain the place of the course in the overall programme. Are your students on a professional translator training programme? When is this course taught, and how does this particular module fit into the overall programme?

Anna Trosborg (Aarhus School of Business): The course is taught in the first year of a two-year MA translation programme. It is taught two hours per week, with 10 weeks per semester, i.e. 20 weeks overall. The aim of the course is to give students a general overview of functions in language and of language theory, that is, insights they will need in the second part of their course where they have courses on technical translation, dealing with economic texts, legal texts, etc. In this first year we use general language texts to introduce the model, and working from English into Danish. The course is optional.

Christina Schäffner: The students you get have a first degree in languages, I assume. Have they heard anything about translation and text analysis before?

Anna Trosborg: They have read something about translation at BA level, and they have done translations before. I also need to add that we base our translation classes on skopos theory. That is, it is generally accepted by the teachers and the students that they translate for a purpose and that this means emphasising the target audience. However, although our students have read a book about textual analysis, they have no practical experience in text analysis. They were translating texts but without a prior detailed analysis. That's why I introduce them to the model with its concepts. This should also help them to deal with the taxonomy in the texts they will come across in their classes on specialised translation.

Peter Newmark (University of Surrey): What do you mean by taxonomy, and what do you mean by a shallow taxonomy in your paper?

Anna Trosborg: Let me explain it by using an example: Take plants, a deep taxonomy is if you start with plants, then you can have flowers, then you can have roses and then various kinds of roses: the more branches in the hierarchy, the deeper the taxonomy. In other words, the deeper you go, the more specialised it will be. Shallow then means you remain at the horizontal level, for example, you go from plants to flowers, and then you look at grains and other parts of flowers, i.e. you are defining different categories.

Peter Newmark: I think that is an interesting concept, but I don't think it is a very useful one in reference to a text.

Anna Trosborg: Texts may develop in different ways. A concept may get introduced into a text and then developed either by going deeper and deeper, or by stopping at a particular level in the taxonomy. So a text may start with introducing the category animal and then go on to speak about birds or insects. Another text may start with the category animal, then go on to speak about dogs, then spaniels, then different kinds of spaniels. If you are reading a text, it becomes clear that the deeper the level of the taxonomy, the more specialised the text. I think it will be good for students to know about these taxonomies. We try to teach them these taxonomies and at the same time we introduce them to the semantic categories: hyponymy, superordinate and subordinate terms. Other semantic concepts we introduce are, for example, meronomy, antonymy, synonymy, i.e. we show students that concepts can be inclusive, exclusive or that they can overlap.

Christina Schäffner: And you say that your students had never heard about these categories and these terms before in their undergraduate programme?

Anna Trosborg: They might have, but we repeat these categories for them. They learn about systems, for example, taxonomies or parts of a machine. The knowledge of these systems might help them identify these systems in another language, and this will also be of relevance for translation.

Peter Newmark: Well, this is semantics what you teach. This all sounds very technical, and I don't think it is useful. You don't need all that to explain the difference between, let's say, 'include' and 'consist of', verbs which are often mixed up in translation. There is neither time nor need in any translation course to go into such depth.

Anna Trosborg: But if you are dealing with technical translation, knowing all the various parts of a machine, and understanding how it works, it should be helpful in the translation. If students don't understand how the mechanism works they could have difficulties. The other problem is that such overlaps and synonymies differ from one language to another. English and Danish do not have the same systems and that's why it is important to know where they differ. We introduce our students to the general theory, and then we go from there to find out about the differences between the languages, that's the main aim.

Rodica Dimitriu (University of Iasi): What I find particularly interesting in your paper is the terminological distinction that you make here, and in other materials that you have published, between genres and text types. This is obviously relevant for translation studies too. Moreover, describing genre conventions is a crucial problem especially for professional translators of non-literary texts. This direction of research still needs to be developed in the future by translation scholars. For example, we keep speaking about textual competence, but we don't know exactly what it consists of and what specific skills to teach for particular genres.

Anna Trosborg: I agree, if you are aware of the conventions of a genre at least in your own language then you can also compare the genres in other languages and see where the differences are. There are certainly cultural differences in genre conventions. We need a clearer knowledge about genre conventions in several languages and cultures.

Rodica Dimitriu: Yes, exactly, first of all we need to have an awareness of conventions that work in our own culture, and then we can compare.

Anna Trosborg: You mentioned terminology. Quite often there seems to be some confusion surrounding the metalanguage that we use to describe features of analysis. For example, what do we mean when we speak of communicative function? How is it different from communicative purpose? What is a text type. What is a genre? Are we speaking about the same things when we use such terms?

Peter Newmark: I agree with you that it is important to do genre analysis, but this was already done by Crystal at least 20 or 30 years ago, when he was describing the characteristics of various genres. There is also nothing very original about skopos theory, which was mainly derived from Bühler's functions of language, although I think the skopos theory is a distortion of Bühler. There is always the danger of consecrating clichés and platitudes and stale language. A translator ought to use fresh language, to use words in the most expressive way possible. You do not get that through standard models of various genres.

Palma Zlateva (University of Leeds): I think it is very useful that you treat genre as something superordinate to register features. But you refer to genre as the purpose of the interaction, and then you speak of genre as activity. I think the genre is a characteristic of the text as a final product, and that the (re-construction of) the meaning of the text as a final product does take into account the purpose, etc., but genre is not a process, it's a kind of a frame, a product.

Anna Trosborg: I do comment on the communicative purpose which is a very problematic issue because the text can have more than one purpose, and quite often there is also a hidden purpose. People who do genre theory take the communicative purpose to define the genre. Genre is taking together field, tenor and mode, and if you have defined these three, then you quite often also have a definition of the genre.

Peter Newmark: I'd define genre as a form or a medium rather than a purpose.

Christina Schäffner: The terms which are used come from various disciplines, and we may or may not apply them with the more or less recognised definition they have in the respective disciplines. We would probably have to clarify all the terms each time we use them. We had a similar debate in the seminar with Mary Snell-Hornby in February 1999, with respect to the notion of cultural identity. Defining the concepts and terms we use is surely very important.

Carmen Rosa Caldas-Coulthard (University of Birmingham): Your basic theoretical framework is systemic linguistics, your taxonomy is from lexical semantics, but then you have speech act theory, you include framing and I assume you took it from Goffman, you talk about Grice, and so on. My question is: Why are you mixing all these different theoretical veins? What is your justification for using all these different terms and theories? What we do is just use one of them, namely functional grammar.

Peter Newmark: It's a rather eclectic model, which is good.

Anna Trosborg: I'm choosing a more mixed model because it allows me to get at as many aspects of a text as possible. For example, I work with Grice because his maxims, especially the maxims of quantity and relation, make a lot of sense to the students. They can use the maxim of quantity to see whether what they can come up with in the source text (ST) is what they want to put in the target text (TT). They can ask themselves: is it enough to keep the reader informed? For example, the reference to Machiavelli in the source text, with reference to the maxim of relation they can argue whether this is something relevant to the readers, whether the term on its own is sufficient, whether it needs to be explained, or whether something more needs to be added. Frames help them to see what's in the text, and it helps them to keep coherence. I quite see that the concepts come from different systems but to my purpose it all makes sense. Based on my experience I would say that a broader model helps the students to do a systematic analysis.

Paul Chilton (University of East Anglia): I'm still a bit confused with respect to your notion of frames. In any case the whole terminology of frames, scripts, scenarios, mental models is pretty confused. Are you using the term 'frame' in the sense of cognitive theory, using work of Schank, Abelson, Minsky, ... or rather in the sociological tradition of Bateson and Goffman? I have the impression you use it in both ways. In your paper you have a reference to a passage from a novel. This passage is used in Paul Werth's book *Text Worlds,* which has a model of discourse-processing which ultimately derives from Fauconnier's mental spaces. This is a fairly technical presentation and Werth's model is perhaps too sophisticated for students. But there are some other issues that have been touched on by Werth in his book, such as reported speech, direct speech and free indirect style (*style indirect libre*), all of which have importance for responsibility and evidentiality. With regard to lexical meanings, I don't think the Hallidayan model is very good at handling that area of language. You referred to a group of words in your sample text, such as *flush out, totter,* ... there are interesting semantic implications in these sorts of cases. How do you train your students to tease out the relevant entailments and connotations?

Anna Trosborg: That's what we try to do by giving them some more semantic theory. We want them to get an idea of what's actually in the text, and they can achieve this by setting up groups of lexical items which are semantically related.

Carmen Rosa Caldas-Coulthard: But this has to do with lexical semantics rather than with framing.

Paul Chilton: It's mainly a terminological issue. Could I also ask about metaphors here: Do you make a distinction at all between what one calls 'embedded' metaphors, metaphors which some people call dead metaphors, which have entered into the structure of the lexicon, and metaphors which are somehow salient? Students need perhaps to apply those or similar terms. Also metaphors very often contribute to the coherence of the text, they can occur in 'chains' in a text.

Anna Trosborg: Yes, we do go into all that when we talk about metaphors, we speak about dead metaphors, conventional and creative ones, and how they function to construct a text.

Paul Chilton: In respect of clarifying the concepts of your model, I'd like to raise a few more points. Although your model is eclectic, there is a lot of Halliday in it. There are some things that the Hallidayan model is not good at, and in particular I don't think it is very good at handling indirect meanings, inferences, presuppositions, entailments, implicatures. In my view students would need to learn something about the nature of indirect meaning. A further point: you talked about the poetic function, derived from Jakobson, and I wondered why you put it in the ideational section.

Anna Trosborg: I put it in the ideational and not in the interpersonal component because it has to do with form and meaning.

Paul Chilton: In Jakobson, the poetic function has to do with orientation towards the message.

Anna Trosborg: Yes, but it's the way the message is being told, the choices you make. That's why it's in the ideational section.

Peter Newmark: Speaking of terms, I think you produced a new definition of intertextuality when you suggest that intertextuality means background knowledge. This is dangerous because intertextuality as I see it means the presence or influence of various texts, either contemporary or historical on a particular text, it doesn't mean just the background knowledge which is cultural.

Anna Trosborg: I do separate intertextuality from culture specific items. Intertextuality is background knowledge required to understand a reference to another text, or several texts. Not all background knowledge is based on another text, a considerable part of it is due to membership in a culture.

Palma Zlateva: A major aim of a model such as yours is to deconstruct the text in order to then reconstruct it convincingly – in a different language. What is evident from the two student papers you showed us is that they do not use this model as a kind of gospel. They have their own variations in the approaches, and they also have different strategies in overcoming the translation problems, which I think is good. I am happy with the approach as such but I have some uneasiness about some of the concepts, which is probably due to the eclecticism of the model. We spoke about genre, but I am also not very happy with this dichotomy between documentary and instrumental translation. You mention interlinear, literal, philological, exoticising etc. as demonstration of documentary translation and you refer to it as a meta-text. In fact, many of those types of translation are not texts at all. A word for word translation does not necessarily result in a text. I would rather see translations like that as a first step, that is, we have to analyse all these elements before we come to the instrumental translation.

Christina Schäffner: The terminology comes from Christiane Nord, it can be compared to a certain extent to Juliane House's covert and overt translation. Nord calls documentary translation that type of translation process which produces in the target language a kind of document of a communicative interaction which happened in the source culture. It's like telling your target readers that the text was meant for the source culture only. However, Nord does not equate documentary translation with an inter-linear version.

Palma Zlateva: To me, documentary translation is going into detail into how the purpose was achieved and analysing the linguistic units themselves, it's more of an inventory of the original text than a meta-text. Popovic talks in terms of meta-text with a view to translation, but he calls the ST a meta- text because this is where you start. You have something general, the meta- text, and this is preserved in all the translations.

Anna Trosborg: What do you think about the two possibilities of translating death columns? I have shown you examples, in one case a translation was produced which is a close copy of the ST, whereas in the other case the target text is adapted to the conventions of a Danish death column. The difference between documentary and instrumental translation comes up quite clearly there.

Palma Zlateva: That's what I would call instrumental translation, the documentary one for me would not be a type of translation at all. With the death columns, you can have an enumeration, a kind of inventory of how it was done in the original. But this inventory does not necessarily even amount to a text.

Christina Schäffner: Oh yes it does, if you apply a functional view of text. You can request such a documentary translation to fulfil a purpose, let's say for language analysis purposes, if, for example, in a teaching situation, you want your students to learn something about the Danish genre conventions of death columns.

Anna Trosborg: You can take any text, even the Bible or literature in general and apply either a documentary or an instrumental translation. That is, the TT produced can be related more closely either to the source culture or to the target culture. We define translation in a broad sense.

Palma Zlateva: If you define it in a broad sense, then I agree.

Anna Trosborg: Normally in translation the genre does not change and, thus, we take genre conventions into account. You can't have an advertisement looking like a cookery book, for example. But there may also be cases where the purpose demands a close reproduction of, let's say, an advertisement. In other cases the advertisement needs to be adapted to the target culture. That's why Skopos theory is so useful.

Peter Newmark: I can't find Skopos theory useful because it has no interest in ethics. Christiane Nord added what she calls loyalty theory, but loyalty only appears occasionally when she thinks that the translator ought to show a bit more respect to the writer than to the customer. How do you teach your students to translate if there are lies in the text?

Anna Trosborg: This is a question which is related to the Gricean maxims, in particular the maxim of quality that is concerned with keeping to the truth. The students are taught these maxims, and we also discuss whether a translator can violate the text, how to act if there is a lie in a text. Skopos theory and Gricean maxims can be combined here. They may be two different things, but it depends on the way you look at it.

Rodica Dimitriu: People are sometimes confused because they make use of different terms to refer to the same things. Then they are not always prepared to accept another definition of a category – for example for genres and text types. Conversely, some terms are used in so many contexts that they seem to lose their significance. I think that the very important category of 'function' tends to be used in too many contexts nowadays. In your model there are ideational, interpersonal, textual functions. We are complaining that the term 'equivalence' covers too many things, and now we have reached a point when 'function' too refers to too many aspects, and thus has become rather vague.

Carmen Rosa Caldas-Coulthard: But Anna is using a terminology from a given framework, a linguistic framework, and these are the concepts used by Halliday. You cannot change the terminology.

Rodica Dimitriu: I agree, but then there are also references to the poetic function and the poetic genre, how do we distinguish between them?

Anna Trosborg: I quite agree that 'function' is a worrying term since it is used in various ways, you can use function for almost whatever you talk about. 'Communicative function' is used in lots of different ways, you talk about 'rhetorical functions', text types, such as narration and description, can be called function. With reference to Bühler and Jakobson you might speak of language functions or of communicative functions. It is indeed disturbing that we need to define the term each time we use it.

Carmen Rosa Caldas-Coulthard: But you can only define a term according to the framework that you are working from.

Peter Newmark: 'Function' is a technical term in mathematics and in one or two other technical contexts. It is also a general word and you will not be able to get rid of it. It means 'purpose', and what would be most helpful is that each time anybody uses the word 'function' they put it in the co-text, use collocations. This might be more satisfactory, but the word is there and it's no good complaining.

Christina Schäffner: It is also important that in the training process we ask our students to read various articles and books by scholars who come from various backgrounds. In this way they can become aware that words like 'function', 'genre', 'meta-text', and 'equivalence' are used differently.

Peter Newmark: The word 'equivalence' is an indispensable word in translation, but it is a general word, it is not a technical word. When people try to produce it as a technical word there's always trouble.

Palma Zlateva: Many terms we use in translation studies come from 'ordinary' language. When you are teaching, when you are trying to show the students as much as you can within the limited time that you have, you need to expose them to various points of view and to different definitions of terms. But in order to call the result 'a model', I think you have to be more consistent in using the terminology.

Peter Newmark: Your model is eclectic, and eclecticism which means choosing from the best, is always a good thing. Translation as an interdiscipline should exercise eclecticism. But I would like to add another question, namely: what have you left out? I think you have left out all the most important things. I regard all dualistic and consumerist theories of translation, such as Skopos theory, as far too narrow. There are other factors, which I call the five medial factors. Let me just summarise them briefly: (1) Is what the source language text says true (i.e. the factual truth)?; (2) Is it agreeable? I haven't heard this subject mentioned at all today, but it is a very important aspect of Chinese translation theory, for instance. (3) Is it logical? (4) Is it moral? That is, does it conform to the ideas of human rights which any translator, in my opinion, ought to subscribe to. And lastly, (5) the linguistic truth, which I could illustrate by saying should one translate proverbs or idioms which are non-cultural? The translator may have to intervene by commenting on one of the factors, usually extratextually. I can use Hallidayan terminology and a Hallidayan approach to a text, but translation is much deeper. Translation can often criticise something much wider than this or that text. That's why I am saying you left out the most important things in translation.

Paul Chilton: There is something missing in your model for me as well here, namely the question: What is translation all about as a transaction in human societies? From the perspective of critical linguistics or critical discourse analysis we can see translation as a particular kind of social action, and then all kinds of ethical, political and social questions, as well as aesthetic ones come in. And there are more specific questions like: Who is translating for whom?, What is getting translated?, When? and What are the effects on the receiving culture?

Anna Trosborg: All those issues are indeed part of the model, specifying time, place, addressees that's all part of the skopos analysis. My approach is to show what textual analysis can contribute to translation. I don't say that's all there is to translation. And it's also not the only course the students get on their programme. They have textual analysis in their first year to make them reflect. They can then use this model for any text they translate.

The Application of the Model in Translator Training

Beverly Adab (Aston University): What you are offering is a very comprehensive model, a very complete coverage of language functions which I would find very difficult to slot into the time available, also bearing in mind whatever else we want to achieve in a programme. How is your model actually applied by the students in their decision-making processes? I can see that it is very valuable for sensitising them to language functions, for helping them to rationalise choices and develop strategies, but at what point can you see the concrete proof of the application? Is there any kind of post-production analysis that goes on as a way of demonstrating how they applied the analysis that was originally thought out and written up in their pre-translation analysis?

Anna Trosborg: When they go on to the second part of the programme, where they do translation of technical or legal texts, they can use the general concept we are teaching them in detail in the translation process.

Beverly Adab: So you are actually setting them up to do the rationalising, the reasoning and the analysis beforehand, but when they do the specialist translation, are they then required to refer back to the knowledge they have acquired in your course and reflect upon the model?

Anna Trosborg: They are expected to be able to work within the system, but they won't necessarily reflect upon it. The only reflective course is the one I have spoken about, the other ones are practical translation classes.

Beverly Adab: Do you have a feedback loop where you then have some input as to how well the students have performed and how well they have applied the framework you have been giving them?

Anna Trosborg: The only feedback I get is from the paper that they write for my course where they can reflect on the text to translate. We would think that they have understood the main concepts and are able to apply the model, but there may not be a need for a detailed analysis in later courses. The course where I introduce and practice the model is a course in textual analysis, semantics and grammar. It is not just a translation course. That's why a ST analysis is required for the assessment.

Margaret Rogers (University of Surrey): The relationship between reflectivity and performance in translation is probably not a straightforward one. I have noticed that there are students who are excellent translators and also have a high ability to reflect on what they are doing. Then there are students who are excellent translators but have a very weak ability to reflect on what they are doing. There are, of course, those who can do neither, but the relationship I have not yet seen is the ability to reflect at a high level and to be a poor translator. The most common pattern is the rather intuitive translator who has poor reflective abilities. The question therefore is: If you do this kind of detailed analysis as presented by Anna, does it lead to better translators or better translations?

Carmen Millán-Varela (University of Birmingham): I would like to discuss a bit more the relationship between the textual analysis of the ST and the students' performance, i.e. in respect of their actual translation competence. I think it is important to have reflective practice and to make student translators aware of discourse analysis, and in general of language use in culture and society. However, it struck me that in the assessment examples you have shown us, there are 11 pages dedicated to the analysis of the ST, but then the actual reflection on translation strategies were only one page or one paragraph. Perhaps one should move the emphasis away from a detailed ST analysis and instead encourage the students to ask how this model of textual analysis will be applied to the translation. That is, let them reflect on how the model can help to shape the translation and make choices. In that sense we will get a deeper translation process where students are aware and hopefully in control of the choices they make, and where they can also reflect on the effects that their choices may have. Moving the emphasis to a TT analysis and looking at the way students reflect and elaborate their own decision-making process could actually bring us closer to evaluating how successful a model has been.

Palma Zlateva: I may have a partial solution to the problem. What I do in my course is ask the students to do a similar type of analysis of the problems in the texts, but primarily with a view to translation. They write it up and submit it together with the TT. In the assessment, this commentary, which I mark, is one-third of the overall grade. The actual translation is marked by experts in the language, and then I decide on the final grade. Based on experience, I can only confirm that there are people who are not good translators and who can't reflect either, as Margaret has indicated in her categorisation. The grades students come with do not always reflect their real language skills, and students usually want to improve their language when they come to do a Master's programme. Since, however, there is a limit to how far you can 'cover' their language deficiencies, adding a reflective commentary to the translation could be a possibility to combine the two elements, i.e. language training and translation training. How does assessment work in your case?

Anna Trosborg: Half of the mark is for the textual analysis and the other half is for the actual translation. They have to pass both, i.e. if they fail the textual analysis they fail the other part as well. So our exam is not just a test in translation, it's also a test in textual analysis. That's why we put so much emphasis on textual analysis in the course.

Margaret Rogers: I think when we speak about the relationship between the ability to reflect and to translate we should focus more on how one could bridge the gap between the ST analysis and the translation strategy. I'd support Carmen here in suggesting that if you have set the students a particular purpose for the translation, they could also do an analysis of a TT, not their own translation but some model text, some proto-text. A comparison of the two could then bridge the gap a little bit between the analysis of the ST and the translation strategy.

Carmen Rosa Caldas-Coulthard: That is exactly what we do in our programme. What I think is a problem in your exercise is that there is a lot of emphasis on the ST, but there is nothing on a similar generic structure in their native language. I very much support Margaret's suggestion, because on the basis of a comparison they will be aware of how a text functions in a specific social practice and they would be much more competent to produce something that is more relevant.

Anna Trosborg: We do demand this detailed textual analysis but that's not all. We also advise them to do a skopos analysis, both of the ST and the TT, which is part of the students' papers. They do a specification of the ST skopos, a specification of the TT skopos, and then they compare the two. The whole textual analysis is aimed at finding out what is in the ST and then deciding how to translate it, whether we need to reproduce the same meaning in the target language or whether we have to deviate. With the sample text (*Not quite across the Rubicon*), for example, students were working with the model, going through the list (see Appendix to the paper), deciding on answers for the ST and then for the TT. They found out that the difference lies only in the target readers being maybe a little less well educated, but otherwise the parameters remain the same. The next question they have to ask is how can we best achieve a translation that is very close to the ST, because that is what the skopos demands in this particular case.

Carmen Rosa Caldas-Coulthard: And if you do such a skopos analysis there is no need for a discussion such as whether there is a similar metaphor. Or, does this metaphor need to be translated or not?

Tolu Akintonde (Institute of Linguists): I don't think I agree. Translators are supposed to think all the time of the target audience, and this also means you have to think about an equivalent translation of a metaphor or another element from the ST into the TT.

Carmen Rosa Caldas-Coulthard: But then you are back to a simple decoding – encoding mechanism. We are working at a much higher level and if you are thinking of the register, the variation in register, the variation in generic structure, then it doesn't really matter so much if you reproduce the 'Rubicon' or not.

Christina Schäffner: I very much agree. Decisions depend on the cultural context and the function of your text. The danger of such a very detailed analysis is that you might want to go as deep into the ST as possible and then make decisions for the TT solely on the basis of the ST. You might get stuck and think about reproducing a metaphor, that is, you remain at the micro level and forget about skopos and reader and so on.

Carmen Rosa Caldas-Coulthard: That is, you did all the analytical work before, but when you get to the production phase, you are stuck with word for word equivalence.

Beverly Adab: What I'm missing in the samples of your student papers is an explicit account of how they reflected on text-type conventions. They say as a result of their analysis, the field, the mode, the purpose are the same, although I wouldn't agree that the purpose is the same in this particular case. There doesn't seem to be any evidence of reflection on changes that will need to be made in view of different text-type conventions. It's as though they are assuming that because the purpose is the same the format will be the same. It is the retrospective function of your model that seems to dominate over a prospective function. If you don't bring in a prospective analysis students may get bogged down in the retrospective analysis and not project towards the target audience.

Anna Trosborg: I agree that the text type is very important. The approach you need is different, whether you translate literature, or a newspaper text, or a legal text. It is part of the aim of my course to make students aware of this, although it may not be so evident in their papers which I used for illustration.

Carmen Millán-Varela: What is the students reaction to the model?

Anna Trosborg: In the beginning they normally have difficulties, because it is all new to them, but at the end they are very happy with it. They can take it and apply it to any text, and very often they want to write their thesis applying the model. In the course of time, they become very reflective on the way they translate. They are quite aware of what's in the ST and what is relevant for the audience they are translating for. They take the purpose into account when they reflect on how to tackle the various metaphors, the imagery, etc. They think about much more than what we see in the papers.

Steffen Sommer (Aston University): How do you explain that this year the examination results were so much better than the year before?

Anna Trosborg: More training, more emphasis on concepts, I suppose.

Steffen Sommer: I see why you have gone for such an eclectic approach, because for a student who is getting into translation, those concepts are quite tangible. The students can relate to them, they can identify them in the texts, and they don't see what they do as abstract or too theoretical. I think such a very thorough analysis is an advantage on the one hand, especially if we assume that the students who enrol on the course haven't got a very deep knowledge of all those different systems and concepts at the outset, but they do get into that and get an idea of how to use those concepts. On the other hand, there is the danger of fragmentation. That is, students might be very good on the theoretical side and able to relate those concepts to the text, but then they are not able to translate the text appropriately.

Is There a Need for Genre Analysis in Translator Training Programmes?

Christina Schäffner: One problem certainly is whether we have the time to do such a detailed textual analysis, but another question is: Do we actually need to do it? Translation scholars who do not come from a linguistics background would find such a very detailed linguistic analysis of the ST irrelevant. Other scholars, who have come to translation from a background in linguistics, text linguistics or discourse analysis obviously want their students to understand concepts such as ideational or interpersonal function, i.e the Hallidayan model. So do we think we need a module on linguistics and/or text analysis?

Carmen Rosa Caldas-Coulthard: I would say yes, we do need it. We have an MA in translation studies which spreads over three terms and which includes a number of languages. In the first term, students take an obligatory course of 20 hours on describing language, i.e. basically systemic linguistics. In the second term we have a course on discourse and translation where we apply all the basic theoretical topics to translation. That is, we are doing something very similar to what Anna is doing, and I think we are very successful.

Rodica Dimitriu: The course we teach at the University of Iasi is at undergraduate level and combines theory with practice. In the theoretical parts we cover the main directions and introduce trainees to some key concepts in translation studies. Practice mainly consists of translating texts according to specific translation briefs that are closely connected with the particular theoretical aspects dealt with in each course.

Margaret Rogers: Our one-year, two-semester, postgraduate diploma/MA programme includes text analysis, translation theory and translation practice. We start with less specialised texts in the practical translation modules, to give students a context in which to start thinking about the concepts introduced in the more theoretical lectures. Theory and practice modules run in parallel, because students often feel that if they are not doing translation they are not really learning anything. In addition, they have background lectures in the subject areas which they are translating. So we link up the subject knowledge with the translation practice as well as translation theory. We hope that by the end of the course they understand the relevance of translation theory and text analysis for translational competence.

Palma Zlateva: The success of combining theory and practice also depends on whether or not you can be language specific. At my previous university in Bulgaria our work was language specific, with the pair English and Bulgarian. All undergraduate students have translation classes with increasing difficulty of the texts that are being translated from and into English throughout their study. We introduce general translation theory in their third year, and then we split into literary and non-literary translation, discussing theoretical aspects first and then applying them in translation practice. With literary translation we again split after two semesters into film translation, children's literature, etc., so students can specialise. Since I was teaching both theory and practice, I knew quite well the capabilities of all my students and I could advise them as to their specialisation.

For our MA in Leeds, we start with an introduction to translation theory, which is a full module, 20 credits, in the first semester. But here we work with students who come from different linguistic and educational backgrounds, and therefore we have to work on a more general level. We are trying, probably not with great success, to bring in various elements into this module, a bit of linguistics, a bit of semiotics, how to write a research paper, etc. The module thus may become a bit patchy. In addition, students do a module on machine-assisted translation, and then in the second semester we have another more theoretical module, investigating translation, for those interested in theory. They continue with machine-assisted translation, and all the while they do practical translations in the different departments. The problem is, however, that we don't have sufficient control of the teaching there, because the lecturers in the language departments very often don't have a theoretical background in translation studies.

Christina Schäffner: I think this is a general problem. When we set up post-graduate programmes in translation at universities, we must make sure that the teaching is not a continuation of language teaching with translation exercises as it was done at undergraduate level. We should make sure that the people who are teaching on such a programme also have some background in theory, preferably that they are also research-active in translation studies. At least there should be meetings to coordinate the approach to apply, for all those involved in teaching on these programmes.

Margaret Rogers: Talking to colleagues at translation conferences who are responsible for programmes in translation it seems that coordinating between the theory and the practice is a very common problem which is not unique to the UK. And if you offer specialist translation in a range of language pairs and directions, then you are bound to bring people in from outside, whether from outside your department or from outside the university, which again increases your coordination problems.

Anna Trosborg: I think when it comes to translation practice, both our teachers and the students work within the framework of Skopos theory. Our problem lies in the fact that our students do not have enough background in linguistics. I would like to have a separate course in functional grammar for one semester before we start with translation since that would help quite a lot. But since we don't have it we cover linguistic theory as part of the translation course.

Carmen Rosa Caldas-Coulthard: But isn't the actual problem what you want to achieve at the end? I think this is the crucial question. Depending on what you want to achieve you have to do either a lot of linguistics or you do something else. What we want to achieve in our course is a lot of language awareness, and we want to give the students a lot of fundamental tools they can work with later on. But we are not controlling their translation processes, on the one hand because they are done in the language departments, so we have a similar problem as Palma was describing, and on the other hand we also don't have the time to do so. This was the path we chose due to our aim. If, however, you want to concentrate on the practicalities of translation then you don't need to do what Anna is suggesting.

Beverly Adab: In our programmes at Aston, we try to do both. However, there are only a few people involved in delivering the programme, and those of us who teach theory also teach translation practice. In this way we have total control over the approaches applied, and the students can become aware of an on-going link and transfer between the theoretical framework and their performance in practice. One of our aims is to develop students' translation competence on the basis of reflective processes. When evaluating their competence we therefore want to see how much of the theoretical framework they've internalised and how they have actually applied it to the translation task.

Carmen Rosa Caldas-Coulthard: But your situation is much more ideal. Since we have Japanese, Chinese, Greek, German, Spanish and other languages we simply do not have the resources or the people to check the end product.

Beverly Adab: But should we be farming out this kind of applied practice if we have no control over the approach to methodology? Does that not undermine the value of analytical frameworks, or of models such as the one proposed here?

Margaret Rogers: The discussion here again raises the question about the relationship between reflectivity and performance in translation. We therefore return to the question: Does this kind of detailed analysis lead to better translators or better translations?

Paul Chilton: I have the same question: Do the students really need all this apparatus in order to be successful, effective translators? If they do need some of it, how do we decide where it has to be focused? If you think of a particular expertise, for instance, a particular professional knowledge base, like law, or medicine, there is nothing really in Anna's model about that. Does your programme provide any courses on social, cultural, political and historical background?

Anna Trosborg: Specific information about, for example legal systems, economics and politics, is provided in the other courses that follow. That's linked to LSP-translation.

Rodica Dimitriu: In my view, ST analysis is a useful methodological procedure, particularly in translation programmes carried out at an academic level. Such an analysis can be more or less exhaustive, we can use more or less detailed models, but the principle as such works and we shouldn't give it up.

Christina Schäffner: I don't think that anybody has actually suggested that ST analysis should be given up. I think the question we have is how detailed does the analysis have to be, do I need to do all these things which are in the model? My worry is that if you try to get as much as possible out of the ST, then you forget that you are doing this analysis with the aim of producing a translation. It is a translation-oriented ST analysis, and not an analysis of a text as we might do in a discourse analysis class, where we are only concerned with the text as a text in its own culture. Some textual aspects, such as presuppositions and cultural background, are relevant for the addressees of the ST in the source culture situation, but they may not be equally relevant for the TT. I'm not arguing that we don't need any ST analysis, but the question is: How deep does it have to be, and with which purpose do we do the analysis?

Tolu Akintonde: I would like to comment on this from my own experience, I work for the Institute of Linguists and I am in charge of the Diploma in Translation examination. This examination is set at postgraduate level, and for one paper the candidates have to do a translation as well as write annotations on the examination. What Anna is doing in her analysis, is very similar to what our candidates have to provide for the annotations that we require. I find that what your students did in their analyses was very well done, and that's the kind of analysis our candidates would need to do for my examination. I agree that there is also a tendency to get bogged down in a lot of ST material, but I'd say that is very useful. They need to know all the particular aspects in the source text in order to produce the TT. If they can analyse the ST properly they'll find that they can bring all this into their translations, and they are thinking about their audience at the same time. They use their annotations skills which are applied to the ST in such a way that they write good translations. Although I'm arguing for a detailed ST analysis, I'm not saying we should go into every metaphor, for example, but you do have to think about equivalences for the target audience. I would suggest that your students' analysis could actually be split into three parts, the ST, the translational analysis, and the TT. And since they have to think about the target audience at the same time, their analysis is not based solely on the ST.

Anna Trosborg: That is indeed what we are aiming at, we want the students to relate their analysis to the purpose of their translation. They do have some difficulties in doing that, I have to admit. But that's really what we are trying to teach them as far as we can, i.e. to relate it to what you want with your translation, what you're aiming at. But that's the difficult part with this approach, and it's also a difficult part for the students to do.

Beverly Adab: I think the 'function' of your model is to train students to be more sensitive to the parameters within which they can make creative decisions. And that's its strength; it sensitises students to be aware of the framework within which decisions will be made. Whatever kind of text you are going to translate, there will be parameters, whether they are text-type conventions, genre conventions, social expectations, social taboos or whatever. You have to operate within a framework of constraints and if you sensitise students to recognise all the constraints then they are free to make creative decisions. I think that that's the value of any model, it functions as a starting point.

Carmen Rosa Caldas-Coulthard: Perhaps the term 'model' is misleading. You are using frameworks from a variety of sources and you are putting together some kind of analytical framework. We have been doing exactly the same thing as you have been doing for five years now, but we've never called it a model.

Beverly Adab: Maybe most of us are eclectic and select the best of different models, according to our interests, our focus and our students' needs.

Anna Trosborg: Let me stress once again that what I have presented here, this model, or analytical framework, is just a minor part of the translation course at our university. You shouldn't get the impression that that's the only thing we do. The course I am teaching, which is an optional course, is also a course in textual analysis, textual analysis for the purpose of translation, it's not just aimed at translation. We teach them a bit of linguistics which they can use for translation purposes. It's almost the only linguistics course they have, and that might also justify why we are putting in so much linguistics and textual analysis as we do. In subsequent seminars they can build on what they did in my class, but this is supplemented by other translation courses.

References

Bateson, G. (1980) *Mind and Nature – A Necessary Unity*. New York: Bantam Books.

Bühler, K. (1934) *Sprachteorie*. Jena: Fischer.

Crystal, D. (1971) *Linguistics*. Harmondsworth: Penguin.

Fauconnier, G. (1994) *Mental Spaces*. Cambridge: Cambridge University Press.

Goffman, E. (1974) *Frame Analysis. An Essay on the Organization of Experience*. New York: Harper & Row.

Grice, P. (1975) Logic and conversation. In P. Cole and J. Morgan (eds) *Syntax and Semantics 3: Speech Acts* (pp. 41–58). New York: Academic Press.

Halliday, M.A.K. (1978) *Language as a Social Semiotic: The Social Interpretation of Language and Meaning*. London: Edward Arnold.

House, J. (1976) *A Model for Translation Quality Assessment*. Tübingen: Narr.
Jakobson, R. (1960) Linguistics and poetics. In T.A. Sebeok (ed.) *Style in Language* (pp. 350–77). Cambridge, MA: MIT Press.
Minsky, M.L. (1975) A framework for representing knowledge. In P. Winston (ed.) *The Psychology of Computer Vision* (pp. 211-277). New York: McGraw-Hill.
Nord, C. (1997) *Translating as a Purposeful Activity. Functionalist Approaches Explained.* Manchester: St Jerome.
Popovic, A. (1980) *Problemy khudozhestvennogo perevoda* (Problems of literary translation). Moscow: Vysshaia shkola publ.
Schank, R.C. and Abelson, R.P. (1977) *Scripts, Plans, Goals and Understanding*. Hillsdale, NJ: Lawrence Erlbaum.
Werth, P. (1999) *Text Worlds: Representing Conceptual Space in Discourse.* London: Longman.

Discourse Analysis as Part of Translator Training: Does It Work? How Do We Set About It? A Response to Anna Trosborg

Beverly Adab
Institute for the Study of Language and Society, Aston University, Aston Triangle, Birmingham B4 7ET

Sensitivity to Textual Structure and Purpose

Most translation scholars who are also involved in university translation studies or translator training programmes are likely to agree on the importance of raising students' awareness in relation to the different ways in which linguistic structures, lexical items and rhetorical devices all serve to reinforce the communicative purpose of a written message or text. Coherence and cohesion are integral aspects of a text of which students need to be keenly aware, in the quest to achieve intended impact and fulfil the purpose of the text. It also involves being aware of the primary factors of the translation situation, from a functionalist perspective, namely the translation *skopos* and the addressee. Knowing the *skopos* is essential, as a first step: only then can the translator determine the needs of his or her addressee in relation to the message to be transmitted and make decisions with regard to the extent of the addressee's knowledge of the situation of the message, the field, the cultural context and other relevant aspects. Awareness of all of these will be needed by the addressee, in order to access the full message in the way intended by the skopos.

Most translator trainers would also accept that in their future professional capacity, students are very often likely to be required to work from a source text (ST), making whatever changes, adaptations or transitions are deemed necessary in order to produce a *functionally adequate* target text (TT) (Nord, 1997) – that is, if they are lucky and their expertise is recognised.

This being the case, it is usual practice to expect to expose students to different kinds of (source) text types, each of which will also contain examples of a range of different translation problems, in accordance with the four problem-type categories proposed by Nord (1991, 1997). Translator trainers aim to inculcate in students an awareness of the need to understand fully the ST message, by reading the ST from the perspective of the (prototypical) native-speaker addressee. Only then can the translator begin to determine how best to tackle the process of translation in relation to the intended ST message and the way this fits, or does not fit, with the intended TT skopos. This involves getting 'inside the skin' of the ST message, identifying how the SL author constructed the text, *what* choices were made and *why*, also *how* all the different micro-units work together to form a coherent whole. Sensitising students to how a text has been constructed not only enables them to focus on various aspects of the SL message. It also trains them to be more aware of the nuances of how language works in a 'purposeful' manner (to paraphrase Nord 1997) and hence to be more 'purposeful' at the point of decision-making and selection from different possible translation alternatives, in relation to units of meaning of the SL message.

Hence it would appear indisputable that discourse analysis as a discipline has much to offer students in this aspect of their training, in sensitising them to language as a communicative tool and in helping them to be more selective in how they use language in translation. The question remains – how can this work and how best can we use the concepts offered by discourse analysis, within a functionalist approach to translation?

The Role of Reader Expectations

One fundamental tenet of the functionalist approach is that the message, in the form of a written text, does not rely solely on use of language at the level of micro-units. It also depends for its reception and acceptance on a certain degree of conformity to the expectations of the intended addressee. These expectations will relate to the relevance of the information contained in the message to the reader, to his/her knowledge of the domain, also to his/her immediate and potential (perceivable) needs for information. They will also relate to the degree of intertextuality between the TT and other texts of that type, for that purpose, in the target language culture (TLC).

Within this approach, the decision-making process is therefore and necessarily *prospective*, since the translator will aim to produce a text which will be acceptable to the TL addressee. Acceptability is determined by a range of factors, including the extent to which aspects of the SL message have any meaning in the TL cultural context. Another important feature in message reception, through the medium of a written text, is the TL native-speaker's preconceptions of what features a text will need to have in order to be recognisable as belonging to a certain text type or genre. Discourse analysis needs thus to be complemented by an approach based on text linguistics, so that the translator can not only recognise key features of the ST, but can also predict whether or not these features will be relevant and/or necessary in the intended TT in relation to the skopos for that text. The framework of standards of textuality, adapted by Neubert and Shreve (1992) from the work of de Beaugrande and Dressler (1981) offers very useful concepts and 'labels' for this purpose. The value of giving students a metalanguage comprising relevant labels with which to describe textual features or aspects of the process of translation is well-documented (see, for example, Delisle, 1998; Delisle *et al.*, 1999). It would be helpful to offer clear definitions of the 'labels' used in this framework, including some attribution of sources where well-known definitions are used and a clear indication of where use in the framework differs from the standard (accepted) use of that term.

How Useful is the Proposed Model?

The model presented offers a comprehensive framework to be used by students to develop and document, through the end-of-course assessment, their awareness of features of the SL message. It seems more reasonable to describe this as a framework of guidelines for ST analysis, since the use of the term 'model' might imply a different approach, an as yet unseen set of principles, something new. That is not to say that the 'model' offered is not relevant or useful, simply to state the need for some clarification of the intention of what is being offered and of its intended use.

To offer a framework is a relevant tactic, which is replicated in many disciplines where some kind of performative action is fundamental to the discipline. Nord (1991, 1997) offers a very useful set of guidelines, described specifically as a framework for Translation-Oriented Source-Text Analysis. For the framework offered by Trosborg, criteria for analysis of textual features are presented. From the intended perspective of the usefulness of this framework for training translators, one advantage is that it enhances the reflective process and raises awareness on the part of the trainee of the very deliberate nature of any act of text production, including selection from alternatives, choice or rejection according to predetermined aims within a given framework and approach, for a purpose as defined by the TT skopos.

The 'model' itself has been described as 'eclectic'. This is a perfectly reasonable and widely used approach to the formulation of a framework of guidelines, well within the intentions of skopos theory, whose motive is precisely to remind the translator that there are many different ways of deciding how to deal with types of translation problems. This is also typical of the discipline itself. Translation Studies (TS) prides itself on its overarching scope, on the way in which it draws on other disciplines to improve our understanding of the processes of translation but also to enhance performance in the task and thereby raise the overall quality of the product as the outcome of process and performance.

The model as presented is, quite reasonably, *selectively* eclectic, reinforcing comments made by many TS scholars. Our approach to translator training will inevitably reflect and be influenced by the discipline in which we may have started our research or in which our research interests most closely lie. The model draws on models proposed by others, mainly from a linguistic approach to discourse analysis. One concern is the omission of any reference to the contribution of text linguistics to a more global type of discourse analysis, one which is more specifically tailored to translation as a process leading to an outcome, rather than to discourse analysis as an end in itself.

A further point which is not clear from the model, as applied in the examples of student work presented in conjunction with the paper at the Aston seminar, is the extent to which trainee translators might realise that this process of ST analysis is but the *first* stage in the translation process. Neither was it specified *how* the students would exploit the findings of this analytical process in the actual decision-making stage of the translation process. It was somewhat confusing to find that the students appeared to see the TT skopos as becoming clear as a result of the process of ST analysis. This may be due to the fact that, for the student papers offered as examples, no skopos was stated at the outset of the written analysis.

Given the aim of using discourse analysis as a *pre-translation* comprehension tool, it would be more helpful to train students to begin by stating the skopos of the TT. This would then focus their reading of the ST in a more purposeful way, seeking only to highlight those aspects of the ST which might be relevant for the production of the TT. If students undertake a full analysis of the ST without 'tailoring' their observations to the potential problems for TT production, they might run the risk of producing a TT through retrospective reflection on the ST, rather than through prospective consideration of the addressee and the TLC as primary determinants of the process and of the choices to be made.

One of the major objectives of training translators is to enable them to develop insights into potential problems of translation in a given situation using a given ST to produce a TT for a specific purpose. Another is to help translators acquire sets of potential *strategies* for dealing with differences between the two situations of text production, what Nord (1991) calls the 'rich points'. Chesterman (2000: 82) defines strategies as 'well-tried, standard types of solution to a lack of fit between goal and means'. He also talks of the need for translators to develop awareness of these different (re-usable) strategies, so that an individual can 'access his or her conscious rationality *at will*' (Chesterman, 2000: 79). It is clear that this type of framework can play a significant role in achieving these aims. It may, however, be more effective to ensure that application of the framework to ST analysis is seen as a *first stage*, to be complemented by *prospective* considerations and then by *retrospective* reflection on the TL choices made and the reasons for these. This latter stage is often usefully enacted through the (retrospective) writing of annotations in which the trainee translator justifies choices of solutions to specific problems, by reference to aspects of the SL message and to aspects of TS theory which enabled him/her to select the appropriate TL choices. As I have argued elsewhere, '[c]ritical evaluation demands reasoned argument to justify decisions and can lead to a more self-aware and critical approach to translation' (Adab, 2000: 227).

In conclusion, the model is certainly relevant and offers a useful approach to training translators in how to read the source text. It may benefit from some more specific indications on how this analysis is then used within the translation process leading to production of an adequate and acceptable TT.

References

Adab, B. (2000) Evaluating translation competence. In C. Schäffner and B. Adab (eds) *Developing Translation Competence* (pp. 215–28). Amsterdam and Philadelphia: Benjamins.

Chesterman, A. (2000) Teaching strategies for emancipatory translation. In C. Schäffner and B. Adab (eds) *Developing Translation Competence* (pp. 77–90). Amsterdam and Philadelphia: Benjamins.

de Beaugrande, R.A. and Dressler, U.D. (1981) *Introduction to Text Linguistics*. London: Longman

Delisle, J. (1998) Le métalangage de l'Enseignement de la traduction d'après les manuels. In J. Delisle and H. Lee-Jahnke (eds) *L'Enseignement de la Traduction et la Traduction dans l'Enseignement* (pp. 185–242). Ottawa: Les Presses de l'Université d'Ottawa.

Delisle, J., Lee-Jahnke, H. and Cormier, M.C. (eds) (1999) *Terminology of Translation, Terminologie de la Traduction, Translation Terminology, Terminologia de la Traduccion, Terminologie der Übersetzung*. Amsterdam and Philadelphia: Benjamins.

Neubert, A. and Shreve, G.M. (1992) *Translation as Text*. London: Kent State University Press.

Nord, C. (1991) *Text Analysis in Translation*. Amsterdam: Rodopi.

Nord, C. (1997) *Translating as a Purposeful Activity. Functionalist Approaches Explained*. Manchester: St Jerome.

A Few Remarks on some Key Factors in Analysing Source Texts: A Response to Anna Trosborg

Rodica Dimitriu
'Al. I.Cuza' University of Iasi, Department of English, B-dul Copou 11, 6600 Iasi, Romania

Introduction

One of the issues that arose after Anna Trosborg's key presentation at the Aston University seminar was related to the amount of time that an elaborate model for source text (ST) analysis, such as the one she suggested, might actually take if applied for each and every text to be translated in class. The question was asked not because anyone was in doubt about the benefits of ST analyses for translational purposes, nor because the method is not used in translator training. It was just a way of bringing into discussion the different academic contexts in which translator training takes place, the variety of objectives and levels of such programmes as well as the thorny issue of the number of hours devoted to translation theory and practice, which varies widely among institutions of higher education. I did not provide any detailed comment on the issue at that time, as I thought it was somewhat extraneous to the main purpose of the seminar, as it had been outlined in the speaker's presentation. However, under the present circumstances, an answer to the question could perhaps be used as a commonsensical preliminary remark to the topic of this paper. Once a model of analysis has been described to students, if there is time pressure – as it mostly seems to be the case – its detailed application may actually be done on one (or just very few) text(s) for complete demonstration. Afterwards, only the 'salient features' that offer particularly relevant insights into the translation process could be retained for in-depth class discussions. These 'salient features' are never the same and, besides, the trainer has the possibility to select her/his texts so as to bring to the fore constantly renewed constellations of relevant factors. As to more detailed investigations, they can always be undertaken by students for their examinations either as preliminary ST analyses or as a more rigorous form of providing translation annotations. My position of compromise – probably similar to others – is nevertheless justified by a relatively high number of translation classes, which allows me to insert such (concise) preliminary analyses before any translation proper.[1]

Extratextual Factors: Which are They? How Broadly Defined? How Important?

There have been several attempts to create models of ST analysis and evaluation, and nowadays trainers may resort either to the largely known ones[2] or try to re-arrange these factors according to their own views with regard to their importance. Most contemporary models draw on insights from pragmatic, functionalist and linguistic perspectives, with more or less particular biases towards one of these disciplines or another. The pragmatic and functionalist perspectives place the text within broader situations and contexts[3] that considerably enhance and refine the translator's understanding of the ST. There are, nevertheless, different opinions among scholars as to which particular factors should be incorporated at the extratextual level of the discussion. Whereas most models include *place* and *time* as pertinent features, the *sender* and her/his *intention* – treated separately or not – seem to be favoured mostly by skopos theorists and functionalists.[4] In other cases, these elements may be part of *Tenor* (Trosborg) or be referred to as the *textual* features of *intentionality* and *situationality* (Neubert), in the same way in which the category of Reader is, again, related to Tenor (Trosborg) or is textually inscribed as Acceptability (Neubert).

Function, the element that guides and orients the translation process and accounts for the choice of particular strategies, plays an essential role in Nord's model (e.g. Nord, 1991, 1997). Trosborg prefers to make use of *genre* at this level, as this category covers the communicative function of language, but is also related to structure.

The cut-outs of extratextual elements operated by scholars differ in their *degree of specificity* as well: some models consist of *clusters of extratextual features* gathered under more generalising labels referred to as context of situation, situational dimensions, socio-cultural context, while some others more minutely choose to treat every element in isolation.

One of the more problematic issues is, however, whether extratextual factors actually refer to external situations or to (macro-textual, linguistic) contexts. Whereas Nord's model, by its very choice of elements, seems to favour the former, Trosborg's framework of analysis (like House's or Kussmaul's) could probably be ranked closer to the latter. Besides, not all scholars are prepared to assign equal importance to extratextual factors. The analysis of the socio-cultural situation, which is generally (too) briefly dealt with in pragmatic models, could play, at least for some categories of texts, a more decisive role in guiding ST reading and subsequent translation. The preliminary 'documentation phase' in translator training could involve in more explicit ways disciplines such as history, sociology, cultural studies, as well as more specific subjects, obviously relating to the field and genre of the ST under discussion, in order to develop to a higher extent the students' extratextual knowledge, triggered by the particular text with which they are dealing. It is at this level of analysis that pragmatic and 'ideological' trends in Translation Studies (TS) could meet, in an undertaking tending to integrate any subject-related knowledge that might contribute to clarifying the meaning of the ST.[5]

Internal/Supposed Situations

Besides the extratextual factors that are part of the external situation, the concept of 'internal situation' introduced by Nord in order to distinguish real settings from imaginary ones, and/or real senders from 'secondary' ones, is not only a means of reinforcing the boundaries between factual and fictional texts[6] but also a way of tracing a textual map that highlights the areas to which 'real' situational criteria could be applied. Internal situations are therefore intratextual, 'the necessary information on the situational factors [being] usually given within the frame text' (Nord, 1991: 41). Turner (1973) also speaks of 'supposed situations' with reference to fictional texts:

> If a supposed situation is extensively developed in a coherent way, it acts in the way that circumstances act in shorter speeches, to provide a context for each of its component details. This is the basis of fiction; a world is built up in words and this world becomes the context in which each sentence has its meaning. [...] A supposed situation differs from circumstances in being a timeless artifact, a shaped world, analysed and yet contemplated as a whole. (Turner, 1973: 139)

Both concepts could be made use of when dealing, for instance, with varieties of language in fictional or in framed texts or when accounting for an author's particular style.

A main criterion according to which trainers could build up or choose a framework for ST analysis, could actually be its capacity to approach, through adequate, text-sensitive instruments, both factual and fictional texts, even if – as is mostly the case – translation programmes are not designed for literary translators.[7]

Text Types and Genres

The different angles of investigation of both text types and genres – linguistic, pragmatic, rhetorical, text-linguistic, functionalist – have led to their different definitions and descriptions of their relationship, hence the different ways of dealing with them in ST analyses. Reiss (e.g. 2000) and Nord regard text types mainly in the light of their communicative function, as illustrations of the (interplay between) fundamental functions of language,[8] which are correlated in their turn, by Reiss, to translation methods. Text genres or varieties refer to 'linguistic characteristics or conventions' (Nord, 1991: 34). Many other definitions of genre bring into discussion matters of convention or draw on associations with literary texts. The fact that text types or genres as distinct categories for analysis are not present in Nord's model may point to their subordination to *function*, which is a cornerstone element in her analysis. In Trosborg's model, *genre* becomes a distinct factor. It is not subordinate either to register or text type, which actually cut through it. Thus, register concerns the immediate situational context of any text (definable through field, tenor and mode), and text types are approached and classified from a rhetorical perspective as narrative, descriptive, argumentative and instructional.[9] Genre is defined from a different theoretical perspective as 'a staged, goal-oriented, purposeful activity in which speakers engage as members of our culture' (Martin & Rothery, cited in Trosborg, 1997: 8, passim). The examples in the model of genres whose variation is correlated with the variation of the situational dimensions of field, tenor and mode, clearly show that literary genres are just one category from a wider range of possibilities.

It is certain that *genre*, in the (useful, productive) acceptation in which Trosborg uses the term, deserves special attention in ST analyses, and translator training could gain a lot if more accurate descriptions of genres were available. A possible advantage of using the term 'genre' in its broad sense, instead of 'text type', concerns the *cultural* associations that it entails. The ignorance of these cultural conventions is a constant source of covert errors in translation. As Kussmaul puts it, without actually using the term 'genre' but referring to the same aspects (1995: 83),

> it would be very helpful if ... conventions and the differences between conventions in the source and target language were known. For this reason we should encourage corpus-based contrastive studies. ... Eventually we might be able to construct prototypes of text types, as suggested by Neubert ... and these prototypes could then be used for creating textbooks and other teaching material, and they might even be used in computer assisted translation in much the same way as terminology data banks.

Although there is still a lot of research to carry out in the field of genre and text type, things have already developed a lot along the lines 'predicted' by Kussmaul (only) in 1995.

Functions? Features?

Present-day models of ST analyses assign, and quite understandably so, a key role to the concept of function. Functionalist approaches draw on the definition of this concept provided by the Prague School of Linguistics, relating to the purpose of communication. As an extratextual factor that must be dealt with before the translation proper – the function of the ST has first to be compared to the prospective one of the target text (TT) – *function* is a dynamic element, which may frequently change when addressing texts to different cultural and linguistic communities. Nord's classification of translations as documentary and instrumental is also related to the functions these types of translation fulfil, the fundamental criterion for distinguishing between them being whether the function of the TT is different from the one of the ST or not, with all the ensuing translation strategies that both variation and invariance entail. Besides, Nord attempts to refine the functions fulfilled by documentary and instrumental translations by examining several possibilities according to the purpose and focus of each translation.

In House's model, as well as in Trosborg's, functions are referred to as texts in a given situation (characterised by field, tenor and mode), the source for function taxonomies being Halliday. House speaks of cognitive-referential functions as well as of interpersonal functions, whereas Trosborg mentions ideational, interpersonal and textual functions, using this category interchangeably with 'features'. On a micro-level, she mentions the communicative functions of speech acts, whereas the poetic function is part of the ideational function of language.

The use of the category of *function* in the different contexts – the ones shown above as well as others – is well justified by the claims of the (functional(ist), pragmatic and linguistic) theories that various scholars have developed. Yet, the problems that may arise when making use of the term in various contexts within the same model are of a methodological order. The term may lose its considerable didactic potential through overuse. As 'function' is a concept which is particularly useful when accounting for human communication, it is extremely important for all disciplines focusing on this aspect. Still, the excessive use of this (fashionable) word may run the risk of making it become so general as to cover almost anything at any level of the analysis thus depriving it of its didactic significance.

Conclusion

The remarks and comments I have made on some factors that I regard as being of particular importance for ST analyses with a view to translation are meant to reinforce my (experience based) belief in their methodological efficiency for translator training. The references to several such models already in use do by no means support one model to the detriment of another. They have been just means of bringing to the fore some problematic issues in undertaking ST analyses, the different ways in which scholars have tried to cope with them, as well as my own tendencies towards sketching out a model of analysis that is broad and flexible enough to incorporate all text-types (or genres, in the sense in which Trosborg defines the term) and all the elements that might be pertinent to the translator's work of interpreting ST meaning. In order to attain this purpose, functionalist, pragmatic and linguistic insights need to blend with socio-cultural ones in an investigation that combines textual analyses with (bolder) inquiries into the extratextual events that generate texts and contribute to their reception.

Developing an awareness of the aspects that need to be taken into account in order to achieve communicatively successful translations is, to my mind, an unavoidable 'explicit' stage in translator training.[10] Even when professional standards are reached, and intuition comes to play a more important role in translating, the documentation phase in the more flexible forms it may take remains an important part of the professionals' jobs.

Notes

1. In this paper I mainly have in view the prospective use of such models, deliberately leaving aside more specific aspects relating to their retrospective evaluative potential, which could form the object of a separate debate.
2. This paper will mainly refer to the models applied by Trosborg (this volume), House (1977), Larose (1989), Nord (1991, 1997), Kussmaul (1995), as well as to some of Neubert's textual features (e.g. 1996). This limitation does not diminish the importance of other insights into the matter.
3. Delisle *et al.* (1999) notices the distinction that is sometimes made between 'linguistic context' and 'extralinguistic situation', a distinction that I take into account when dealing with these terms.
4. Not everybody claiming functionalist affiliations (i.e. House, Kussmaul, Trosborg, etc.) would, however, incorporate them into their models or, if they do, they tend to blur other differences like the ones between intention, function and effect on which Nord (1991) insists on.
5. During the documentation phase of the translation of a culture-bound contemporary short story, while analysing the extratextual factors of *medium* and *motive* (cf. Nord's model) my students decided to write to the author, feeling it was the easiest (possibly the only) way to clarify some intratextual matters relating to these elements. Thus, they found that the short story was mostly dialogue because it was a written text meant to be read on the radio (*medium*) and the incorporation of Bernstein's *West Side Story* into both the structure and content of the text was due to the fact that the short story was also a tribute to the great composer and conductor's merits shortly after his death. These pieces of information entailed further translational decisions. Students wanted their text to be 'performable' as well, thus paying particular attention to the register they chose, sentence structure, particular illocutionary force of the speech acts they dealt with, etc. As to the 'Bernstein tribute', they decided they could make use of

the information by adding a footnote when the name of Bernstein's musical occurred for the first time in the text. I refer in more detail to this documentation phase in translation elsewhere (Dimitriu, 1997).

6. As Nord (1991) shows, secondary senders may exist in factual texts as well, in newspaper articles for instance when an opinion is quoted.
7. Yet, the expressive function which predominates in literary texts exists in other categories of texts as well and needs to be practised in translation programmes. Trosborg takes account of it in her model, when she very specifically refers to the poetic function of language.
8. As is known, both Reiss and Nord – among others – make use of Bühler's classification of language functions as referential, expressive and 'appellative', to which Nord adds Jakobson's phatic one (Jakobson, 1960).
9. This classification is taken from Hatim and Mason (1990) and is also mentioned in Larose's (1989) model.
10. This is referred to as stage 3 ('the competence stage') in Chesterman's (e.g. 2000) description of stages of expertise.

References

Chesterman, A. (2000) Teaching strategies for emancipatory translation. In C. Schäffner and B. Adab (eds) *Developing Translation Competence* (pp. 76–89). Amsterdam and Philadelphia: Benjamins.

Delisle, J., Lee-Jahnke, H. and Cormier, M.C. (1999) *Terminologie de la Traduction*. Amsterdam and Philadelphia: Benjamins.

Dimitriu, R. (1997) Pre-translational activities and the translator's options. In K. Klaudy and J. Kohn (eds) *Transferre Necesse Est* (pp. 303–09). Budapest: Scholastica.

Hatim, B. and Mason, I. (1990) *Discourse and the Translator*. London and New York: Longman.

House, J. (1977) *A Model for Translation Quality Assessment*. Tübingen: Narr.

Jakobson, R. (1960) Linguistics and poetics. In T.A. Sebeok (ed.) *Style in Language* (pp. 350–77). Cambridge, MA: M.I.T. Press.

Kussmaul, P. (1995) *Training the Translator*. Amsterdam and Philadelphia: Benjamins.

Larose, R. (1989) *Théories Contemporaines de la Traduction*. Québec: Presses universitaires de Québec.

Neubert, A. (1996) Textlinguistics of translation: The textual approach. In M.G. Rose (ed.) *Translation Horizons – Beyond the Boundaries of Translation Spectrum* (Translation Perspectives IX) (pp. 87–106). Binghamton, NY: State University of New York at Binghamton NY, Center for Research in Translation.

Nord, C. (1991) *Text Analysis in Translation*. Amsterdam and Atlanta: Rodopi.

Nord, C. (1997) *Translating as a Purposeful Activity*. Manchester: St. Jerome.

Reiss, K. (2000) *Translation Criticism – The Potentials and Limitations – Categories and Criteria for Translation Quality Assessment*. Manchester: St. Jerome.

Trosborg, A. (1997) Text typology: Register, genre and text type. In A. Trosborg (ed.) *Text Typology and Translation* (pp. 3–23). Amsterdam and Philadelphia: Benjamins.

Turner, G.W. (1973) *Stylistics*. London: Penguin Books.

On Models, Visibility and Translation Pedagogy: A Response to Anna Trosborg

Carmen Millán-Varela
Centre for English Language Studies, University of Birmingham, Birmingham B15 2TT

Translation, Linguistics and Pedagogy

In spite of the controversy around the influence of linguistics in Translation Studies, it is undeniable that linguistic and textual approaches have a key role to play in translator training, particularly those approaches which incorporate social, pragmatic and discoursal factors. However, the assumed relevance as well as the central position given to these approaches is usually based on the theoretical orientation of the lecturers imparting the courses, and not enough on empirical evidence of their appropriateness as translator training tools. It is therefore becoming painfully evident that a pedagogical debate should be accompanying the implementation of (linguistic, literary, computational, etc.) models which attempt to improve translators' competence and performance. Lack of pedagogical reflection in this area reveals the still underlying assumption that translation equals language acquisition, and which is probably responsible for the continuous disagreements and mistrust about the 'usefulness' of linguistics in translation studies, as a whole.

In a similar way to previous existing models (Hatim & Mason, 1990; House, 1977; Nord, 1991), Trosborg's 'eclectic' model constitutes another effort to apply a linguistic-textual analysis to a translator training programme. The model reshuffles and reorganises categories already used in various models by organising them into 'extratextual' and 'intratextual' elements. I could argue about the suitability of the categorisation, or point out absences, as well as unnecessary elements. However, as one of the aims of this debate was to improve the quality of student education, I would like to adopt a pedagogical stance and draw attention to those elements which lack visibility in this model, namely the translating process, students' voice and the pedagogical implications. House points out that

> any attempt to teach translation competence is premised on the assumption that one knows what translation competence is. Therefore a theory of translation and of translation quality assessment must underlie any pedagogic training. (House, 1997: 167)

Reflecting on Trosborg's model, the absence of the pedagogical element becomes obvious. The underlying assumptions about translation in this model seem to be influenced by skopos theory and Nord's ideas, although it is not entirely clear what 'translation competence' or 'translation quality' mean here. Considerations on translation are reduced to issues of 'equivalence' and they appear after the presentation of the linguistic component, somehow disassociated from it. Thus, the model, in spite of being qualified as 'process-oriented', is heavily biased towards the source text (ST).

In Trosborg's paper, there is not sufficient information on the actual implementation of the model or on actual results. The linguistic ideas underlying this particular model, as well as the different components in which it has been structured, are not issues that can be properly discussed if taken in isolation from their pedagogical context, that is, without referring to the aims and learning outcomes. Thus, a series of questions stem directly from my reading of the model, and from reflection on similar models: What type of linguistic knowledge do translators require for their everyday work? What are the differences between training translators and training linguists or text analysts? How can discourse analysis, text linguistics, etc. contribute to the development of competent translators?

Reflecting on Trosborg's Model: Aims, Learning Outcomes, Assessment

From my interpretation of the model, the main concern seems to lie with the articulation of the model and how to fit all the various linguistic and textual components. Although a deep understanding of the ST is, of course, necessary, I do not think it should be considered as the exclusive aim of this type of model. Ultimately, an understanding of the ST will have to be 'translated into' practice. Although I am sure that producing accurate and acceptable translations is an underlying learning outcome of the model, this is not obvious and has not been formulated as the main aim. Kiraly (1995) has pointed out that

> to train student translators, we must first ask what skills and knowledge professional translators have that our students do not yet have and, second, how we can effectively and efficiently create an appropriate learning environment for acquiring such skills and knowledge. (Kiraly, 1995: 2)

Trosborg specifies that the aim of her model is 'to create a deep understanding' of the ST by means of detailed analysis. It is interesting to note the small space allocated to the target end and, in particular, to the students' voice. In this sense, the model appears to be too ST oriented, too concerned with finding the 'right' meaning, with providing 'the' right translation. From a pedagogical viewpoint, Trosborg's model, or rather her aims, do not differ much from more traditional, prescriptive approaches, what Kiraly denominates 'performance magistrale' (Kiraly, 1995). Although the author mentions that emphasis is 'not only on the quality of the product (the translation) but also on administering the process' (in the Introduction), little attention is, in fact, paid to the process. This becomes particularly evident in the assessment method, which takes the form of a one-week writing assignment, namely '12–15 pages of textual analysis, and a translation of a given text'. Trosborg adds that textual analysis and translation are given equal weight and that they receive equal amount of attention during the course. This type of assessment agrees with the initial aim of the course, namely to test understanding of the ST. However, if we wish to test students' use of textual analysis in their translating practices, to assess how textual analysis contributes to improve students' translating performance, then the emphasis should be removed from the ST only and include both the student and the translating process. In this sense, 12 pages of ST analysis seems somehow redundant if a commentary is to be added to the translation. Why not include the linguistic analysis as part of the justification procedures that should accompany the translation? In this way, linguistic knowledge will be seen as part of, and actively shaping, the decision-making process. Commented translations will be useful to access information on how students activate the linguistic knowledge obtained, how they reformulate the data extracted from the ST analysis and the problems they face. These commentaries would constitute relevant information to assess the success and appropriateness of the model used. Has the model actually contributed to a better understanding of the (English) ST? How have students applied the (linguistic, textual) knowledge acquired when faced with the task of translating a particular text?

We have not been given detailed information regarding teaching methodology, or how the model has been implemented in the classroom, or about students' reactions. Although specific details on English–Danish may not have been relevant here, as the author suggests, some discussion on the strategies or activities used to encourage students to reach appropriate solutions would have been useful. In the concluding comments, Trosborg provides some interesting information about students' behaviour and 'bottom-up' approaches, when she says 'Students may be tempted to keep as closely as possible to ST structures, which is likely to lead to linguistic interferences and mistakes even when translating into the native language' (in Concluding Comments). Students 'forgetting' what they have been taught or reverting to 'wrong' practices, what does this tell us about the model, about students' needs? I think this is an extremely relevant observation, which should be further researched in order to ascertain the validity of the model in use. Due to the vast amount of information to be covered in this module, and considering its practical orientation, a student-centred, problem-solving methodology seems the most suitable option. The linguistic component therefore would not be taught 'in a vacuum' but embedded in the course according to students needs.

Final Note

Linguistic approaches should not be viewed as exclusive mechanisms to 'enter' texts but as useful instruments to support textual understanding *and* (re)production. They are tools which students can use to cope with complexity and difference, to justify their own translating options, and to measure the quality and validity of their own products. In view of these comments, I would rephrase the aims of the model so that it not only aims at a deep understanding of the ST but also at the production of accurate and acceptable texts in the target language. Otherwise, it would not be necessary to include a translation exercise as part of the assessment. As a result, methodological and assessment changes will have to take place accordingly. Visibility and target-orientedness, two concepts which have been crucial in the theoretical development of Translation Studies, also need to find their way into the translation classroom. It is obvious that there is another gap that still needs to be filled.

References

Hatim, B. and Mason, I. (1990) *Discourse and the Translator*. London: Longman.
House, J. (1977) *A Model for Translation Quality Assessment*. Tübingen: Narr.

House, J. (1997) *Translation Quality Assessment a Model Revisited*. Tübingen: Narr.
Kiraly, D. (1995) *Pathways to Translation. Pedagogy and Process*. Kent, OH: Kent State University Press.
Nord, C. (1991) *Text Analysis in Translation*. Amsterdam: Rodopi.

The Deficiencies of Skopos Theory: A Response to Anna Trosborg

Peter Newmark
Centre for Translation Studies, School of Language and International Studies, University of Surrey, Guildford, Surrey GU2 5XH

Anybody would agree that you need to know why you are doing something, as well as what you are doing and how you are to do it, and that sometimes if you get too involved, you tend to forget what your aim is. Hence the *Bauhaus* follows the convolutions and intricacies of *Art Nouveau*. But to translate the word 'aim' into Greek, and make a translation theory out of it, and to exclude any moral factor except loyalty, added on as an afterthought by Nord (e.g. Nord, 1997) to Vermeer (who wrote that the end always justifies the means, (e.g. Vermeer, 1978), is pretending too much and going too far.

'Although the distinction between "semantic" and "communicative" may appear similar to the notions of "documentary" and "instrumental", the two approaches are widely different in their focus', says Anna Trosborg (section 3.1.2). She is right there, but how are her readers/students to understand her, when she makes no proper reference to me, my books or my other published work in her lengthy and overly didactic, not to say prescriptive, lucubrations? Her analysis of the distinction, however, is misleading: 'documentary' translation, which is Nord's term, not Vermeer's, reproduces, in some form or other, the full content of the source text (ST), whilst 'instrumental' translation normally only reproduces the part related to its purpose, the message. The distinction appears futile, since all translation is instrumental. The distinction between communicative and semantic translation, however, depends on the importance, the purpose and the quality of the text, as well as other factors (see Munday, 2001: 45). Moreover, the 'ultimate determiner' in my model is certainly not 'ST' (I quote Trosborg, Section 3.1.2). It is, as I have explained many times, in the books Trosborg has ignored, one or more of the five universal non-cultural truths (to which I also referred in the Debate).

Further, Trosborg appears to be unaware of any distinction between imaginative ('literary') and factual (non-literary) translation, her own prose tending to frequent repetitions and dead linguistic terms ('commissives', 'representatives', 'declarations') that do not serve translation. She selects the terms of Joos's (1969) scale of formality (a 'consultative' register, for instance, what is that? Trosborg gives no illustrations), which preceded the turn of language towards increasing informality, due to the spread of democracy, TV, the internet, etc. (e.g. an immediate use of first names), that has taken place since that period. She is unaware of the distinctions between degrees of formality, emotional tone and simplicity for these distinctions see Newmark, 2000: 14f.). If her theory of good writing, such as it is, with its slick or 'crucial' strategies, is based on Grice (who is not in her references), she hardly flushes out or relates his principles to any text. Her reference to 'epistemic modality', without definition or example, is obscure and misleading, as is her remark that 'Translation Studies has changed from a preoccupation with literature to a concern with general and specialised language' (Section 3.1); she seems merely to be betraying a prejudice against literature. In fact, writers on translation are as concerned with literary as they are with non-literary language.

Lastly, in her litany of ST pointers, Trosborg omits punctuation marks, typographical modifications, illustrations, diagrams, which are so important as cohesive factors, or as indications of emphasis, summarisation, doubt, irony, etc. In her inadequate analysis of *The Economist*'s style features for a translator, she makes no mention of the illustration at the top of or in the middle of the page (as published in the journal) that normally indicates the point of the article.

In short, I think Trosborg's formulas are dreary and include too many remarks that are not worth making (such as 'we should not expect theoretical models of translation to solve all the problems ...'. [in Concluding Comments] *et patati et patata*), but as a preface to Halliday, I have no quarrel with it.

References

Joos, M. (1969) *The Five Clocks*. New York: Harcourt Brace.
Munday, J. (2001) *Introducing Translation Studies*. London: Routledge.
Newmark, P. (1978) The curse of dogma in translation. *Lebende Sprachen* 23, 99–102.
Newmark, P. (2000) *Text Book of Translation*. Harlow: Pearson Education.
Nord, C. (1997) *Translating as a Purposeful Activity. Functionalist Approaches Explained*. Manchester: St Jerome.
Vermeer, H.J. (1978) Ein Rahmen für eine allgemeine Translationstheorie. *Lebende Sprachen* 23, 95–98.

Text Analysis as a Tool in Translation Training: Why, How and to What Extent? A Response to Anna Trosborg

Palma Zlateva
Department of Russian and Slavonic Studies, University of Leeds, Leeds LS2 9JT

Translation and Understanding

We all seem to agree that the text as an 'isolated, self-contained semiotic formation' (Lotman, 1990: 47) is the basic unit of translation. Very broadly speaking, translation is a process of extracting the meaning of a source text (ST), and rendering it by means of the language units and structures of a target language (TL), preserving (ideally) its message/communicative goal. Such a broad definition poses a number of problems, of course, and we cannot go into all of them now, but being able to analyse a text is undoubtedly a valuable skill for any practitioner of translation.

Extracting the meaning and identifying the message of a text are two aspects of *understanding* it, of *making sense* of it. This ability builds upon the ability to decode its linguistic structure and comprises a basic prerequisite for coping with the task of rendering it into another language. But understanding a text does not automatically result in an ability to recreate it in a different language. Neither do these two processes take place in a discrete and consequential manner, as we translation practitioners and educators know only too well. The process of understanding and creative thinking itself involves translation.

> When we are dealing with discrete and non-discrete texts, translation is in principle impossible. The equivalent to the discrete and precisely demarcated semantic unit of one text is, in the other, a kind of semantic blur with indistinct boundaries and gradual shadings into other meanings. If in these other texts we do find segmentation of a sort, it is not comparable with the type of discrete boundaries of the first ones. Given these factors, we are faced with a situation where translation is impossible; yet it is precisely in these situations that efforts to translate are most determined and the results most valuable. For the results are not precise translations, but approximate equivalences determined by the cultural-psychological and semiotic context common to both systems, *this kind of 'illegitimate', imprecise, but approximate translation is one of the most important features of any creative thinking*'. (Lotman, 1990: 37, my italics)

As the Russian philosopher Gusev points out, the problems of understanding and its status as a universal cognitive process have been addressed by both fundamental sciences (e.g. linguistics, sociology, logics, philosophy and psychology) and applied ones (e.g. translation theory, media communication theory, information and artificial intelligence theories, etc.) (cf. Gusev & Tul'chinskij, 1985: 7).

Within the framework of Parret's views on a theory of understanding, the aspect of understanding that we need to apply to translation itself belongs to the realm of its pragmatics (Parret, 1980, quoted in Gusev & Tul'chinskij, 1985). Understanding a text, or 'making sense' of it, is a creative dynamic process, involving individuals and taking place in certain social and temporal parameters. So, although the ST we subject to analysis is a finished material product, its understanding – let alone its linguistic re-creation in a different socio-cultural environment – is a process that involves much more than an analysis of its linguistic structure. Summarising various hermeneutic views, Gusev defines three types of interpretation: grammatical, stylistic and historical. He points out that the first one is the only purely linguistic type of interpretation, whereas the other two are related to the artistic, historical and personal contexts of the linguistic activity resulting in the production of a text (cf. Gusev & Tul'chinskij, 1985: 34–37). Dridze talks about the dual character of the text: as *a linguistic unit*, i.e. 'a stretch of linearly organised flow of speech', and *as a unit of communication*, i.e. 'a functional, hierarchically organised wholesome unit of meaning and content, related to the communicative and interpretative goals of the subject of communication' (Dridze, 1984: 46–47). Brandes states that

> the training of professional translators cannot be restricted to understanding on the level of sensory-empirical or intuitively psychological knowledge. It demands that they be taught to understand a text in a holistic manner, i.e., to achieve a deep and total comprehension of it, which entails knowledge of its history (both material and cultural), information about the author of the original as an individual and a representative of the culture of a specific period, as well as an ability to logically analyse the text and theoretically conceptualise it. (Brandes, 1988: 20)

We should also bear in mind that

> the understanding of a different linguistic world can never be complete and definitive, not allowing for alternatives. Finally, *this understanding is always guided by a preliminary understanding, defined by one's mother tongue, [a preliminary understanding] which the bearer is not conscious of, since it constitutes an integral part of that tongue*. (Brandes, 1988: 28, my italics)

Language-specific or General Approach to Text Analysis Teaching?

This brief overview seems to answer the question of *why* we should teach text analysis in translation training courses. The questions of *how* and to *what* extent still remain, however, and few authors go beyond the 'a translator should *know* ...' or 'we *should teach* translators to ...' to suggest a consistent and plausible working way of achieving such a goal. I see Anna Trosborg's presentation and the discussion that followed it as a very important attempt to do just this. She presents to her students a variety of approaches to text analysis, modifying some of their elements to suit better the purposes of translation-oriented teaching. For example, she treats the notion of genre as something super-ordinate to register features. But she refers to it as *the purpose of interaction*, and then speaks of genre as *activity*, which I find a bit inconsistent. It seems to me that both when we generate a text, and when we *experience* it (i.e. read or hear it) we place it within the [mental framework] of some kind of genre, and we build or decode it according to the specific rules of this genre. So, *the purpose* of the interaction we have in mind *defines the genre* of the text we are going to produce, and we perform *the activity of speech interaction*, following *the rules of that specific genre*. But genre is not the purpose itself, nor is it the activity or process of generating or decoding a text.

The issue of genre as a set of socially established and culture/rhetoric specific linguistic norms and a kind of mental framework for generating/understanding a text is even more complicated when we talk about translation. As we pointed out, in contrast to the SL recipient of a text, a translator's preliminary understanding of a ST is defined by their mother tongue, which is also the TL in which they then generate the TT. It is my belief that in teaching translation we can and have to use language-specific text analysis, based on this preliminary understanding as a step in the interpretation of a ST which precedes its actual translation into a TL. And this is my very general answer to the question of *how* we teach text analysis to translation students. However, I failed to see it in Anna Trosborg's approach, although she – unlike the majority of those present at the Aston seminar – has the advantage of teaching a homogeneous group of students, working within the pair of the Danish and English languages.

As you may have noticed, I call it an *approach* rather than a *model*. Anna Trosborg introduces to her students different, sometimes even incompatible text-analysis strategies and theories, as was pointed out by a number of the participants in the discussion. It is this eclecticism that prevents me from considering her approach to be 'a model of text analysis for translation purposes' – although, as Peter Newmark justly pointed out, 'sometimes eclecticism can be enriching' (cf. the Debate). In fact we can see that the two students whose papers we were given as samples, have, indeed, used different approaches to the analysis of the assigned text. They have also used different strategies in overcoming the translation problems which this text presents, which I think is good. However, it is hard to came to any statistically meaningful conclusions about the impact of [the efficiency of] the ST analysis based on the quality of their translations. Or, as Margaret Rogers put it earlier in this discussion: 'The relationship between reflectivity and performance in translation is not a straightforward one ... and we can have intuitive translators with poor reflective abilities'. (I have also had students with very good analytical skills who do not exceed in translation performance – PZ.) She asked whether 'this kind of detailed analysis' as presented by Anna Trosborg will indeed lead to better translators or better translation. This question was addressed to all of us, and I am afraid I cannot give it a firm positive answer at this stage. In order to come closer to such an answer, though, we have to take account of the particular circumstances in which we teach translation, and of the types of students/courses we teach. What works and brings good results in the type of course Anna teaches, or the type of course I taught back at 'St Kliment of Okhrid's' University of Sofia, cannot work in the MA in Applied Translation Studies at the University of Leeds – or at the University of Birmingham, judging from what Carmen Rosa Caldas-Coulthard said earlier during the Debate.

In my old Sofia university, a course giving an Introduction to the Theory of Translation is taught as an obligatory course in the first semester of the final under-graduate year of English (and other modern languages). All our students also do linguistics (both theoretical and English) and literary theory, so they are familiar with the basic theories in these fields and their terminological apparati. When they proceed to their postgraduate level, they have the options of doing courses in literary translation, non-literary translation or interpreting. Among those who specialise in literary translation, I could then select about half a dozen – those who have demonstrated good skills in dialogue translation – and teach to them a module in Film Translation. The rest can either continue with [an advanced course in] literary translation, or opt for a module on Translating Children's Literature. This is a very consistently and exhaustively structured course working within one pair of languages only – a luxury which only a few, if any of us teaching various types of postgraduate courses here in the UK, can afford. In the majority of cases, MA programmes in translation continue for one year and are taught to a mixture of British and international students, coming from different educational and cultural backgrounds. Some of them have not studied any linguistics, semiotics or semantics, let alone discourse analysis or rhetorics, so offering them 'this kind of detailed text analysis' is simply impossible. It can be done – to a certain extent – in an optional module only. For example, I introduce some elements of text and discourse analysis in a second semester module I teach, called Investigating Translation.

A Process Model as a Tool to Teaching Translation

For practical courses in translation, or for courses to 'clients' of the type I have just described, I would prefer an approach of the type recently presented by Jameson as a tool to teaching Russian–English translation (cf. Jameson, 2001: 8):

Process model	The process model is intended as a teaching guide listing the sequence of points which need to be discussed (or decisions that need to be made) in logical order in order to define translation priorities which will be used to resolve translation dilemmas when translating.
	Questions for class discussion
1. Cultural context ⇓	(1) What is the date of the text? What historical period is referred to? What were everyday life/social/political conditions like then? Did e.g. transport and the media differ then? Are local customs referred to?
2. Text type ⇓	(2) Is the genre indicated? If not what do we judge it to be? What are the characteristics of the genre? Does this genre exist in England? What are the markers that indicate this text-type?

3. Function of text

⇓

(3) What function does this text have in the source language (SL)? Why is it being translated? Who is the intended target language audience? What use do they want to put the text to? Does the TL text's function differ from the SL text's function? How?

4. Translation priorities

(4) The needs of the target audience should define translation priorities. What form should the definition take? Should we list several priorities if so in what order?

5. Tone

(5) Are any sections of the text ironic or humorous? Have they included attributed or unattributed quotation from a third party? Have we missed any of these?

6. Formal problems

(6) What formal problems have been included in this text? How do we solve them?

7. Checking procedures

(7) Compare the length in words of SL and TL phrases. If the TL version is longer can it be shortened without compromising our goals? Has the principle of necessary sufficiency of explanation been applied?

Jameson, too, calls this approach 'a model' – a term almost as abused in Translation Studies as the term 'theory' – although to my mind it is a simple working algorithm of text analysis. He works within one language pair, Russian to English translations. It is my belief, however, that his approach, being much simpler, is also more universal and can easily be refined and/or adapted to the text types and language specific problems within different other pairs of languages. And it can, hopefully, be at least a partial answer to the question *to what extent* should text analysis be taught to translation students.

Conclusion

In this brief addition to the discussion based on Anna Trosborg's paper on Discourse Analysis as Part of Translator Training, I have tried to put the need to study the ST structure in the broader context of understanding a text. I have also outlined some of the problems that have to be solved by any translation scholar who aspires to create a model of text analysis for translation purposes. I grouped those problems around the major questions of *why*, *how* and *to what extent* we need to teach text analysis to students of translation. I have also offered to the readers' attention a practical approach, used by a colleague of ours from Lancaster in his translation classes with English speakers of Russian. Finally, I would like to thank Anna Trosborg for providing us with such an interesting material for discussion, and I would also like to thank all colleagues who shared their valuable experience and theoretical and methodological observations in an attempt to improve the quality of teaching of translation.

References

Brandes, M. (1988) *Stil' i perevod (na materiale nemetskogo yazyka) [Style and Translation (on Material from German)]*. Moskva: Vysshaya shkola.

Dridze, T. (1984) *Tekstovaya deyatel'nost' v strukture social'noi kommunikatsii [The Textual Activity in the Structure of Social Communication]*. Moskva.

Gusev, S. and Tul'chinskij, G. (1985) *Problema ponimaniya v filosofii [The Problem of Understanding in Philosophy]*. Moskva: Partizdat.

Jameson, A. (2001) A practical approach to teaching Russian–English translation. Paper delivered at the 9th BASEES conference. Cambridge, 7–9 April 2001.

Lotman, Y. (1990) *The Universe of the Mind. A Semiotic Study of Culture*. London and New York: Tauris Publishers.

Getting the Balance Right: Some Concluding Comments on the Responses

Anna Trosborg

The purpose of my seminar was to discuss my approach to textual analysis, to access its validity as an analytical tool and its value as a tool in translator training. I encouraged the participants to respond critically and give their personal views based on their experiences, so we could have an interchange of ideas, share ideas on pedagogical issues and, eventually, maybe even arrive at an 'ideal approach'. This resulted in a lively discussion and furthermore, in five written responses. I would like to thank all who took the trouble to respond to my paper for the valuable insights put forward in these papers. In my response, I will concentrate on important points highlighted by the respondents, just as I will clarify and comment on some of the points where there seems to be misunderstandings or disagreements.

I am glad that you all agree that the ability to analyse a text is undoubtedly a valuable skill for any practitioner of translation. Textual analysis is an important step in understanding a text and as pointed out by Beverly Adab, 'it also enhances the reflective process and raises awareness on the part of the students or trainees of the very deliberate nature of any act of text production, including selection from alternatives, choice or rejection according to predetermined aims within a given framework and approach, for a purpose as defined by the TT skopos'. Sensitising students to how language can be used to achieve a communicative purpose and to produce a text which is appropriate to the TL audience is an important part.

Acknowledging that textual analysis is an important tool in translator training, the question is then 'why, how and to what extent'. This question is taken up and discussed by Palma Zlateva. This is an important point, do we really need such a detailed model as I presented, or can we do with simpler versions? My experience is the same as Palma Zlateva's: in ordinary courses we do not have the time to do detailed analyses of all aspects, but such analyses can be undertaken with great success in optional courses. At the Aarhus School of Business, the course in question is also optional, a point which I seemingly have not made clear enough in my presentation. However, most students take the course as a basis for subsequent translation courses in specialised language where textual analysis is not an explicit part. The course which combines textual analysis and translation gives the students who attend an opportunity of analysing a text in great detail and of reflecting on aspects of translation considerations for which there is hardly any time in ordinary courses. They consider the acquired skill of great importance, they find that it creates an awareness of many aspects they would not otherwise have considered, and many students follow the approach if they choose a translation task as their MA thesis.

Palma Zlateva contributes with a presentation of a process model by Jameson, which is less time-consuming and which may well be used in ordinary translation classes. Each course is, naturally, to be adapted to its specific students and their needs.

Another solution to save time is Rodica Dimitriu's suggestion that we start explaining our model in full and apply it to a few texts, but thereafter select 'salient features' that offer particularly relevant insights into the translation process for in-depth class discussions. These 'salient features' differ from text to text, and the teacher then has the possibility of selecting texts that bring up constantly renewed constellations of relevant features. In fact, I see it as a very important point to train students to see which features of a textual analysis are relevant and which are less important to a particular translation task, so they learn to select just these features without having to go through the model as a whole. But this needs thorough training and can only be done when students are confident with the detailed model. When this has been achieved, students may begin to focus their reading and their analysis of the ST in a more purposeful way, seeking to concentrate on those aspects of the ST which are likely to be relevant for the production of the TT. In this respect, an initial focus on the TT skopos will be very helpful, as emphasised by Beverly Adab.

The socio-cultural situation is indeed to be thoroughly analysed, as suggested by Rodica Dimitriu, just as a preliminary 'documentation phase' could explicitly involve disciplines such as history, sociology and cultural studies. My students are always encouraged to analyse the socio-cultural situation as closely as possible. Besides, I urge students to find all cultural expressions (and intertextual references) in a text in order to pay particular attention to these expressions in the translation process. They must consider the importance of these expressions and their existence (or lack it) in the target culture (TC). If there is no translation equivalent, the student knows s/he has a problem which needs particular attention. Knowledge of both the ST culture and TT culture is a very important aspect, and it is my experience that students are willing to do some research in relation to this point, in particular if they are dealing with texts of some length and/or importance. They are well aware that this is an important aspects if they are to live up to the demand for communicatively successful translations. And, as pointed out, this documentation phase in its more flexible form remains an important part of the job also for professional translators.

I am glad that Rodica Dimitriu agrees with my distinction between genre and text type as the two have often been confused. Knowing the conventions of a genre is indeed important in translation, in particular as these conventions may differ from one culture to another. As she puts it, 'ignorance of these cultural conventions is a constant source of errors in translation'.

Carmen Millán-Varela also acknowledges the influence of linguistics in translation studies: 'it is undeniable that linguistic and textual approaches have a key role to play in translator training, particularly those approaches which incorporate social, pragmatic and discoursal factors'. At the same time she points out that a 'pedagogical debate should be accompanying the implementation of (linguistic, literary, computational, etc.) models' which attempt to improve translators' competence and performance. She further states that lack of pedagogical reflection in this area reveals 'the still underlying assumption that translation equals language acquisition, which is probably responsible for the continuous disagreements and mistrust about the 'usefulness' of linguistics in translation studies, as a whole'. The view that translation studies should equal 'language acquisition' is long outdated, as the focus in translation studies for a long time has been on communication. The value of linguistic theories for translation purposes varies, I think, with the extent to which they are integrated in the process of text production.

I fully agree that pedagogical debates and pedagogical reflection are very important issues not to be forgotten in any translator training programme. Nor has it been forgotten in my approach. It is true that Part 1 of my paper is concerned mainly with textual analysis, as the aim of this seminar was indeed to access the value of the presented approach as one way of analysing a text as preparation for a translation. It is not true, however, that the approach is heavily biased towards the ST. Part 2 is devoted to translation strategies and Part 3 to translation strategies for one particular text. Moreover, the model consists of three parts: A, textual analysis; B, consideration of TT (translation skopos); and C, translation strategy, translation, translation comments. In addition to my position paper, two full papers (40 pages) of students' application of the model, including: *textual analysis, comparison of ST skopos and TT skopos, outlining of translation strategies, translation and translation considerations and comments* had been distributed to all colleagues attending the Aston seminar beforehand. From these papers, it is obvious that the students do indeed include the textual analysis as part of the justification procedure for the selection of linguistic material in their translations.

The pedagogical aspect is certainly very focal in the approach. Throughout the course, the students were encouraged to relate their textual analysis to considerations concerning their translations, and thus to use their findings (linguistic, socio-cultural and textual) to justify their translation decisions. 'The students' voices' echo in their papers, just as these papers are evidence of the actual implementation of the model and of the results of applying it. After each section in their textual analysis, the students comment on the value and consequences of the outcome of the analysis for their considerations and choices when translating, and it is evident from these papers that to a great extent they draw conclusions from the analysis that are useful in the process of translating the text.

To come back to the point raised by Rodica Dimitriu concerning the importance of sociocultural factors, this is just one of the aspects where the outcome of the analysis is explicitly discussed for each item in the students' translation comments. Consideration of cultural differences lead to considerations of where to adapt, comment on and sometimes even ignore aspects of the ST (if considered of little importance to the TT reader). Thus, I do indeed have commented translations which according to Carmen Millán-Varela 'will be useful to access information on how students activate the linguistic knowledge obtained, how they reformulate the data extracted from the ST analysis and the problems they face'. These commentaries, she continues 'would constitute relevant information to assess the success and appropriateness of the model used'. To give the participants of the seminar an opportunity to apply the model themselves and to scrutinise students' commentaries were indeed the very reasons why two full papers had been put at the disposal of all participants.

Awareness of the primary factors of the translation situation, from a functionalist perspective, namely the translation skopos and the addressee, are among the concerns of Beverly Adab. Students need to know that knowing the skopos of any text is essential, as a first step in the analysis as well as towards text production. The students need to be able to determine the needs of the addressee in relation to the message to be transmitted and make decisions with regard to the extent of the addressee's knowledge of the situation of the message, time, field, the cultural context and other relevant aspects. This is well in agreement with my approach.

Furthermore, she points out that prediction of whether or not the ST features will be relevant and/or necessary in the intended TT in relation to the TT skopos, as well as what other means are at the students' disposal to re-create and achieve the desired effect are indeed very central aspects. Only then can students/translators perform on the ST whatever changes, adaptations or transitions of form, style and textual conventions are deemed necessary in order to produce a functionally adequate target text in agreement with the translation brief. I totally agree with Beverly Adab that knowing the skopos should be a first step in the analysis. Therefore, the task assignment to the students always includes a translation brief or statement of the purpose of the translation from which the TT skopos can be derived. This translation brief or purpose statement is always presented to the students as a first step of their assignment placed before the ST. Information of time, place, addressees and the purpose of the communication should always be available to the students at the very outset, and this is the way all our translation assignments are formulated.

Thus, the TT skopos is not derived from the ST analysis in my approach; in fact, this is normally impossible. Nor is it seen as becoming clear as a result of the process of the ST analysis, as Beverly Adab seems to think. When the students work with the model, the first thing to be considered is the purpose of the translation, its translation skopos. Essential for skopos theory as an approach to translation is exactly that it takes the desired TT as its outset, and initial considerations must be given to the text to be produced. This is a major contrast to previous translation theories, in which the ST has been the point of departure. For convenience, I have placed 'consideration of TT (translation skopos)' after the textual analysis, as a comparison of the ST and TT skopos can only be undertaken when the ST analysis has been carried out. To prevent misunderstandings from arising, I see that I ought to have pointed out explicitly in the approach that the TT skopos is indeed to be analysed initially so it can function as a point of departure for reading and analysing the ST as a preparation for its recreation in the TL.

In response to Peter Newmark, I will comment on one point only, namely the statement that speech act analysis with categories, such as representatives, commissives and declarations are 'dead linguistic items' that 'do not serve translation'. Hatim and Mason (1990) devote a whole chapter (Ch. 5) of their book on discourse and translation to this issue, and they present numerous examples where translating the illocutionary force of a speech act in the wrong way leads to misunderstandings, as for example translating what is a directive in the ST in such a way that it will be interpreted as a representative in the TT. Furthermore, a change of speech act function may be necessary as a result of the change of skopos, but this is quite a different matter. In both cases, though, determining the speech act function is of great importance to construct the TT message as intended and/or required.

Finally, I would like to thank all participants in the seminar for their interest and their contribution to the lively discussion. Also many thanks to Christina

Schäffner for bringing us all together. An interchange of ideas is very fruitful, and I hope that this seminar with its subsequent publication will result in further discussion as well as make people consider and take up aspects which can be fruitful to their research and teaching in their own particular environment.

Reference

Hatim, B. and Mason, I. (1990) *Discourse and the Translator*. London/New York: Longman.